science
KALEIDOSCOPE

a student's guide to
KEY STAGE
3

Pauline Hoyle Chris Lainé Steve Smyth

HEINEMANN
EDUCATIONAL

science
KALEIDOSCOPE

a student's guide to

KEY STAGE
3

HEINEMANN
EDUCATIONAL

CONT

1. Living World

2. Treasures of the Earth and Beyond

ENTS

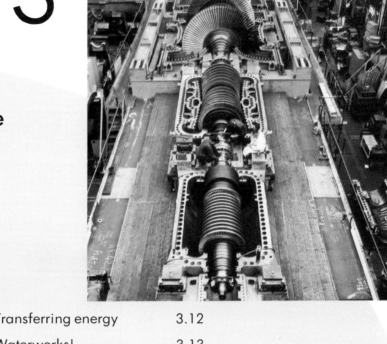

ACID RAIN

Do you think of rain water as fresh and pure? Pure water is **neutral**—neither acidic nor alkaline. It has a pH of 7. Rain that falls in many parts of the UK has a pH of 5.6. Vinegar has a pH of between 3 and 4. **Acid rain** can have a pH of 4—but it has been known to be as low as 2.4. That's more acidic than vinegar! Imagine what it feels like on your eyes.

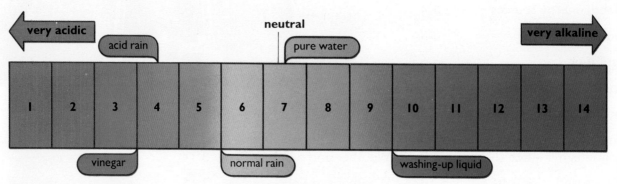

You can use pH paper to measure how acidic a solution is. The colour of the paper tells you the pH

What causes acid rain?

EXPLORE

- List the sources of pollution that produce acid rain. Use the diagrams to help you.
- List the chemicals produced by each source of pollution.
- Draw a map of your local area. Mark on it possible sources of acid rain. (Don't forget to include cars.)

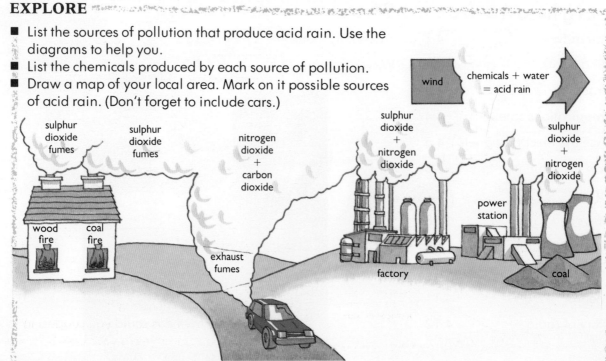

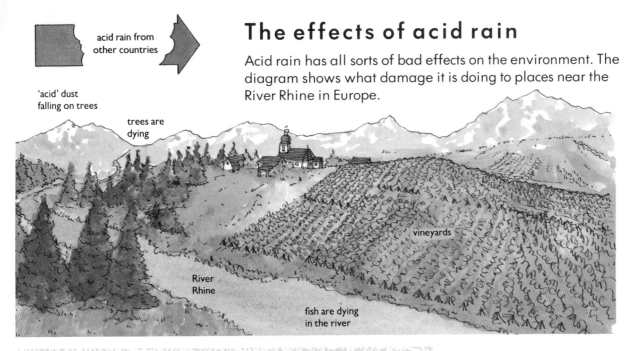

acid rain from other countries

'acid' dust falling on trees

trees are dying

vineyards

River Rhine

fish are dying in the river

The effects of acid rain

Acid rain has all sorts of bad effects on the environment. The diagram shows what damage it is doing to places near the River Rhine in Europe.

PRESENT

■ A neighbour is worried about acid rain and wonders whether he should use an electric fire instead of burning coal. Make a poster to explain the causes and effects of acid rain to him. Use Cut Out LW1 to help you.

How can we help?

Here are some things that can be done to prevent acid rain.

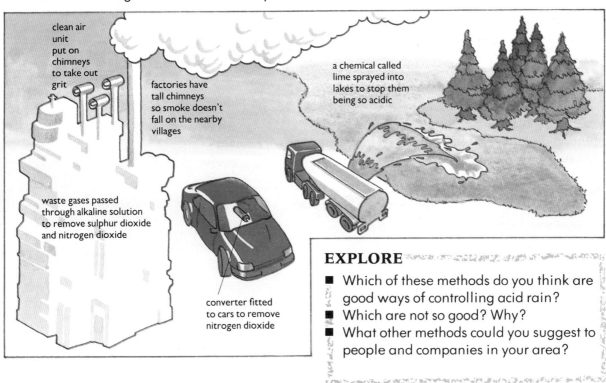

clean air unit put on chimneys to take out grit

factories have tall chimneys so smoke doesn't fall on the nearby villages

a chemical called lime sprayed into lakes to stop them being so acidic

waste gases passed through alkaline solution to remove sulphur dioxide and nitrogen dioxide

converter fitted to cars to remove nitrogen dioxide

EXPLORE

■ Which of these methods do you think are good ways of controlling acid rain?
■ Which are not so good? Why?
■ What other methods could you suggest to people and companies in your area?

ALCOHOL

Why drink?

Alcohol is a drug which is socially acceptable in Britain. People can become **addicted** to alcohol—they can't stop drinking it. People drink alcohol in different situations and for different reasons.

EXPLORE

> John has low alcohol lager during the week, but has beer at a party to boost his confidence.

> Kim has half a pint of lager at lunch time and two glasses of wine each evening. At a party Kim usually drinks 1 or 2 glasses of wine to relax and get in the mood.

> Lucy always goes to parties and is often in the pub—she drinks orange juice all the time as she doesn't like the taste of alcohol.

> Mark usually drinks 4 or 5 pints at parties. He has 2 pints after work every day and 2 whiskies each evening to help him forget work problems.

- What other reasons do you think people might have for drinking alcohol?
- Many people think drinking alcohol is wrong and they would never drink it. Why do you think they feel like this?

Where does alcohol go?

Here are some statements about where alcohol goes inside the body.

EXPLORE
- Make a diagram of the body and add labels to show where alcohol goes. Use Cut Out LW2 (Part 1) to help.
- Make a list of all the organs that alcohol affects.

> The alcohol is absorbed into the blood from the gut.

> First the drink goes down the oesophagus to the stomach and gut.

> If there is too much for the liver to cope with, the alcohol is carried out of the liver in the blood.

> Finally the blood carries the alcohol to the brain, muscles and other parts of the body.

> The blood carries the alcohol to the liver so that the alcohol can be broken down.

1.2

How does alcohol affect the body?

Mr Jackson drinks a lot of alcohol regularly. It affects all the organs it passes through. The more alcohol Mr Jackson drinks, the greater the effect on his body. Some effects are short term—they last for one day. Others are long term—they last for months or years.

EXPLORE

- Which of these effects are short-term? Which are long-term?
- What other effects of alcohol do you know about?
- Add labels to your diagram showing how alcohol affects the body. Cut Out LW2 (Part 2) will help.
- Look back to the party scene. For each person, describe how you think his or her body has been affected by alcohol. You are **applying** what you have learnt.

The party (continued)

PRESENT

- Make a rough plan of three possible endings for this story. Choose one that will have most effect and make it into a poster to discourage people from drinking and driving.
- What advice would you give to each person in the story so that this situation doesn't happen again? Put your ideas on the poster.

BEER AND CHEESE

People have been making cheese and beer for thousands of years. They probably discovered how to do it by accident.

> Ugh! This milk's gone all watery at the top and lumpy at the bottom.

> The lumpy stuff tastes nice.

> I wonder if this always happens when you leave milk? It would be a good way of using milk when Daisy produces too much.

These people were finding out how cheese is made

> The barley's got wet in the rain. It must have been here for days!

> It's gone frothy at the top. It doesn't half-smell funny!

> I wonder what it tastes like?

> It could be poisonous!

> 1 hour later... It doesn't taste bad! If this always happens we could make this stuff and sell it — or invite all our friends round to drink it.

> HIC!

These people were finding out how beer is made

EXPLORE

■ Decide whether the people above are making **observations, inferences** or **hypotheses**.

Making beer and cheese involves **enzymes** and **microbes**. Enzymes are substances living things use to make chemical reactions faster. Do you know the names of any enzymes? Microbes are tiny living organisms that you can only see with a microscope.

An enzyme called rennet is added to make the milk separate

Lactic acid microbes in fresh milk make the milk go sour

PRESENT

■ Use the photos and information to write a newspaper article called 'How cheese is made'.

■ Underline in green where enzymes are active and red where microbes are active. You are **interpreting** the information.

The milk separates into solid curd and watery liquid. The solid curd is milled, salted and shaped

The cheese is left to mature. This means that the flavour and texture will change because the microbes are still active inside the cheese

One more beer

Beer can be made from any cereal crop such as maize, rice, wheat or barley. It is a complicated process . . .

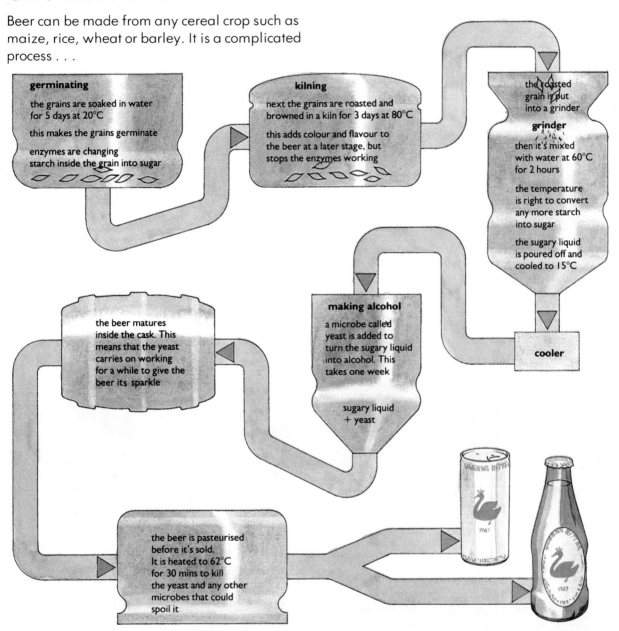

germinating

the grains are soaked in water for 5 days at 20°C

this makes the grains germinate

enzymes are changing starch inside the grain into sugar

kilning

next the grains are roasted and browned in a kiln for 3 days at 80°C

this adds colour and flavour to the beer at a later stage, but stops the enzymes working

the roasted grain is put into a grinder

grinder

then it's mixed with water at 60°C for 2 hours

the temperature is right to convert any more starch into sugar

the sugary liquid is poured off and cooled to 15°C

cooler

making alcohol

a microbe called yeast is added to turn the sugary liquid into alcohol. This takes one week

sugary liquid + yeast

the beer matures inside the cask. This means that the yeast carries on working for a while to give the beer its sparkle

the beer is pasteurised before it's sold. It is heated to 62°C for 30 mins to kill the yeast and any other microbes that could spoil it

EXPLORE

- Draw a table on a *double page* to summarise the brewing process. Use Cut Out LW3 (Part 1) to help you. You are **interpreting** the diagrams.
- From your knowledge about making beer and cheese, what do you think microbes and enzymes do? Make a list. Use Cut Out LW3 (Part 2) to help you.

	Germinating	Kilning			
Diagram					
Temperature					
Time taken					
Enzyme activity					
Microbe activity	None	None			

BIODEGRADABLE

Things that rot and decay are **biodegradable**. Things that do not decay are **non-biodegradable**.

EXPLORE

■ Classify the objects in the pictures into two groups: biodegradable and non-biodegradable. You are **interpreting**. Add your own examples.

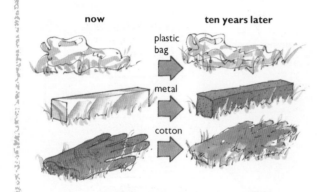

now   ten years later

plastic bag

metal

cotton

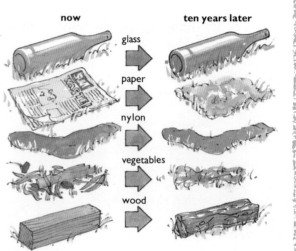

now   ten years later

glass

paper

nylon

vegetables

wood

How are non-biodegradable products used?

floor cleaner
washing powder
detergents
plastic bottles +
packaging

EXPLORE

■ List the uses of each non-biodegradable product in the kitchen shown here.
■ List any advantages of using non-biodegradable objects and any disadvantages. You are **classifying**.

disinfectant
chemical cleaners
bleach

rubbish pit

chemicals that haven't been broken down enter the river

bleach, disinfectants and other household cleaners can prevent the breakdown of sewage

sewage works

car being cleaned with oils and chemical polishes

litter

many marine animals feed by collecting particles suspended in water, including those that are polluting the water. We might eat fish or shellfish affected in this way.

fish tangled in discarded litter

fish poisoned by car oils and solvents

Lemons, vinegar and soda were used as cleaners.

Shoppers took special bags to be filled up by the shopkeeper.

Buckets were metal.

Toys were made of wood.

In the UK people used to use natural biodegradable products ▲

In the 1960s there was a boom in artificial, non-biodegradable products ▲

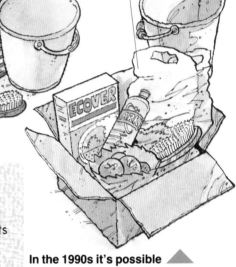

Biodegradable plastic.

In the 1990s it's possible to buy biodegradable materials instead ▲

PRESENT

■ Look at the shopping. List the things made from biodegradable and non-biodegradable products. Why do you think there was a boom in non-biodegradable products in the 1960s? Think about changes you could make at home. Cut Out LW4 (Part 1) will help. Make a poster to remind your family about these changes when they go shopping.

A matter of opinion

Jan's group decided to ask some people what they thought about using biodegradable products. This is what they were told. There are more opinions on Cut Out LW4 (Part 2).

I don't think it will make any difference if I choose biodegradable products. What's the point if no one else bothers?

You have to start somewhere. My dad asked the local shop to sell biodegradable things, and they always sell out first.

I read that there is now technology to make biodegradable plastics and to recycle some plastics. I think the government should give money to this research immediately.

Companies wouldn't make and sell things if they were dangerous. I think they give the public what they want.

I think each person is responsible. People should be free to choose what they want and the government shouldn't interfere.

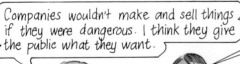

EXPLORE

■ Which factors do you think influence your decisions about what you buy?
■ Use the evidence from the opinions to make a chart like this.
■ Prepare a debate on 'People should stop using non-biodegradable products as soon as possible'. You should have at least six arguments on each side.

Ways the government can influence products	Ways industry can influence products	Ways individuals can influence products

1.4

CHARACTERISTICS OF LIVING THINGS

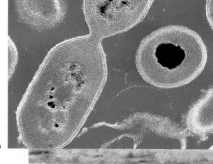

How can you tell whether something's alive? Is an oak tree alive? Is an acorn? Is a table? There are certain things that *all* living things do.

EXPLORE

- What do you think all living things do? Make a list of your ideas. Use reference books to help you.

Bacteria reproduce by splitting in two

PRESENT

- Make a poster for a younger sister or brother to show how lots of different animals and plants do the things you have listed.

Lionesses mark territory by urinating

Trees eventually die and decay

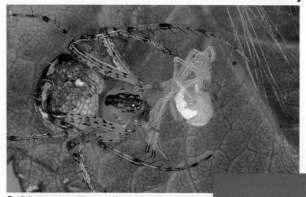

Spiders eat other animals, including other spiders

Dogs breathe hard to cool down

Sunflowers turn to face the sun

Wildebeest run to escape being eaten

There is a very wide variety of living things, but they all share certain characteristics

To do any of the things you have listed, living things need **energy**. They get their energy by the process of **respiration**. Respiration is more than just breathing. It means combining the oxygen they breathe in with the food they've absorbed, to produce energy. This involves the oxygen reacting with many things contained in the food.

One type of food which produces lots of energy during respiration is sugar. Sugar and oxygen react in your body to form carbon dioxide and water, and at the same time give energy to the body:

Sugar + Oxygen ➡ Carbon Dioxide + Water + Energy

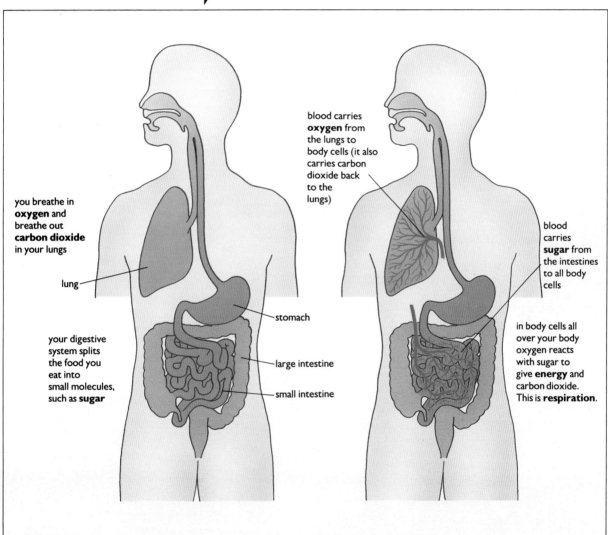

you breathe in **oxygen** and breathe out **carbon dioxide** in your lungs

lung

your digestive system splits the food you eat into small molecules, such as **sugar**

stomach

large intestine

small intestine

blood carries **oxygen** from the lungs to body cells (it also carries carbon dioxide back to the lungs)

blood carries **sugar** from the intestines to all body cells

in body cells all over your body oxygen reacts with sugar to give **energy** and carbon dioxide. This is **respiration**.

These parts of the body are involved in respiration

EXPLORE
■ Make a list of the different jobs that different parts of the body do which make up the process of respiration.

PRESENT
■ Make a poster to explain the reaction between sugar and oxygen in respiration to a six-year-old child.

COUNTRY AND TOWN

According to a recent opinion poll, 80% of the people in Britain want to live in a small country town or a village, rather than in a city.

EXPLORE

- What are the advantages of living in a city?
- What are the advantages of living in the country?
- Would you rather live in a city or the country?

These pictures show the small town of Thatcham in Berkshire. The black and white picture was taken in 1963, the colour photo in 1986. Between 1963 and 1986 the M4 motorway was built and the railway service to London became much faster. A number of important industries have started up in the area.

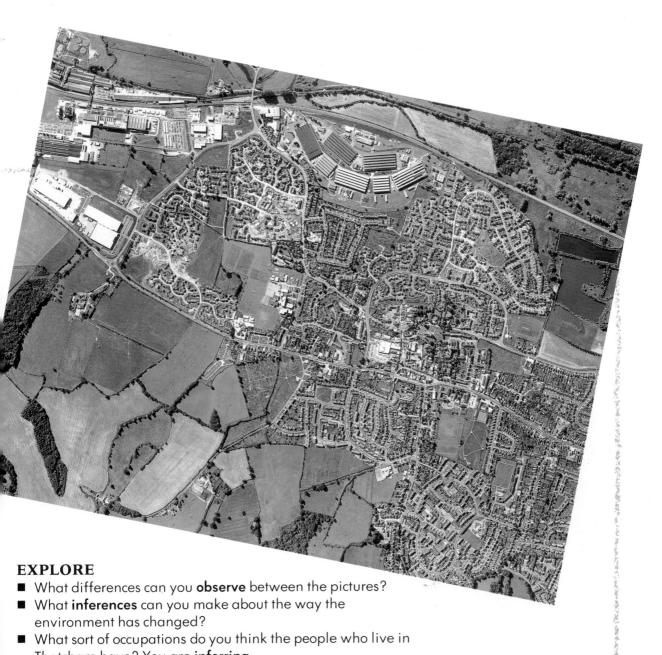

EXPLORE

- What differences can you **observe** between the pictures?
- What **inferences** can you make about the way the environment has changed?
- What sort of occupations do you think the people who live in Thatcham have? You are **inferring**.

This table shows the changes in the number of households in Thatcham and other nearby towns since 1961.

Numbers of households in thousands				
Place	1961	1971	1981	1987
Bracknell	6.0	10.3	17.5	18.5
Newbury	6.5	8.0	9.5	10.3
Reading	49.4	60.7	67.4	76.9
Thatcham	2.3	3.3	5.1	7.1
Twyford	0.8	1.4	1.7	1.8
Wokingham	3.5	6.6	8.1	10.1
Woodley	6.3	10.7	12.7	18.5

PRESENT

- The local council is mounting an exhibition about the development of the area. Present these figures for the exhibition in a way that shows the changes most clearly.

FERTILISER

1 Lee had gone to stay with his cousin Peter, who lived in the country. They had gone for a walk.

Cor! What's that awful smell?

Muck spreading! It's one of the penalties one pays for living in this country village.

2 Lee watched as the tractor sped around the field leaving its trail of smelly gloop.

Whadda they do that for?

3 Peter replied with an air of smug superiority.

The waste products of farm animals contain valuable minerals which can be recycled. That means they're put back in the ground so that plants will grow better.

4 Lee clambered onto the gate for a better view.

Why is it so smelly?

5 Peter once more replied in the tone that irritated Lee so much.

The muck is so smelly because all the old animal protein has been decomposed to ammonia. Plants need nitrogen to grow properly and they get the nitrogen from decomposed animal protein. Don't they teach you city oiks anything? And you'd better get down off the gate before the farmer sees you!

6 Later that day.

I wonder if he'll grow any better if I push him in that? That would make a good investigation.

PRESENT

Back at school, Lee's group were doing some work on fertilisers. Lee told them the story of what happened with Peter, and they also found some leaflets and books.

- Use Lee's story and any information you can find to design a poster explaining what fertilisers are and why they are necessary. Are fertilisers always necessary?
- Devise a play to present these ideas to an accountant who wants to leave the city and start a market garden.

People apply their knowledge about nitrates and plant growth by fertilising the soil. This means adding substances that will make plants grow better. One of the main things added in fertilisers is nitrates, but other chemicals are important as well. Some farmers use fertiliser made up of rotting animal remains, because protein eventually decays to nitrate. Other farmers use fertiliser that is made in a factory – this is called artificial fertiliser.

What's the relationship between nitrogen and protein?

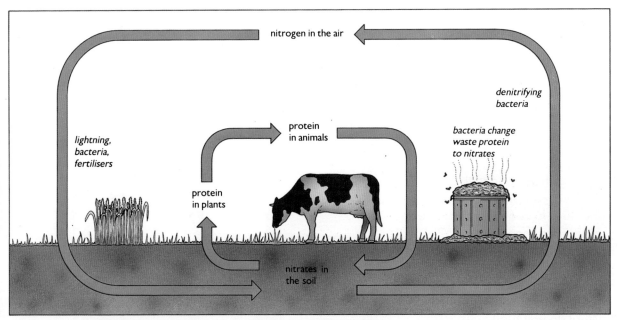

Nitrogen is constantly recycled from the air to the soil and back again. Fertilisers play a part in the cycle. There is more about this on page 1.8.

EXPLORE

- Draw a cartoon strip to show how nitrogen gets from a person to the soil and back again.
- What is meant by a high-protein diet?
- Which foods can you think of which are advertised as being high in protein?

Everybody needs protein. In fact, every living thing needs protein. Protein is a name for a type of chemical. These chemicals are used to build up cells – so bodies are built out of protein.

We get our protein by eating it. Both meat and vegetables contain protein. But where do the animals and plants that provide meat and vegetables get their protein? Animals get their protein either directly from plants, by eating them, or indirectly, by eating an animal that has eaten a plant. But how do plants get their protein?

Plants can make their own protein, so long as they have a starting chemical called a nitrate. Nitrates are simple chemical compounds (you may have seen some copper nitrate in the laboratory). Plants can take them in through their roots.

GOING ROUND IN CYCLES

How is carbon recycled?

EXPLORE

- You have probably heard that carbon dioxide levels are rising. Why do you think this is?
- Why is it a problem?
- Copy the green boxes into your book. Label each line. There are some phrases to choose from on Cut Out LW5 (Part 1).
- Which processes add carbon dioxide to the air? Which processes remove carbon dioxide from the air?
- What will happen to the levels of carbon dioxide in the air if lots of trees and plants are chopped down? What will happen if humans burn large amounts of wood and fossil fuels? You are **interpreting**.
- What do you think will happen to levels of carbon dioxide in the air over the next 100 years? Explain why you think this. You are **predicting**.

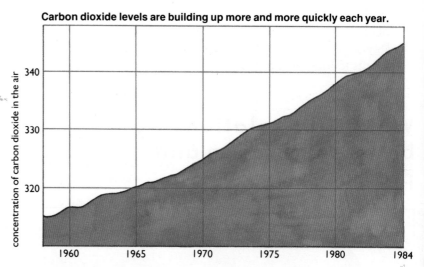

Carbon dioxide levels are building up more and more quickly each year.

concentration of carbon dioxide in the air

340

330

320

1960   1965   1970   1975   1980   1984

The carbon cycle shows how carbon dioxide is formed in the atmosphere, and other places that carbon appears

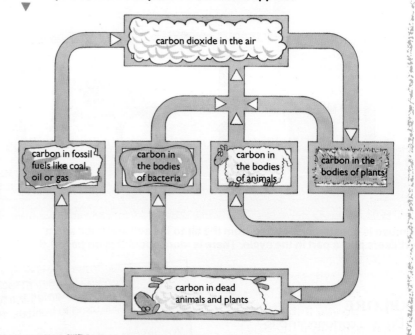

carbon dioxide in the air

carbon in fossil fuels like coal, oil or gas

carbon in the bodies of bacteria

carbon in the bodies of animals

carbon in the bodies of plants

carbon in dead animals and plants

PRESENT

- Imagine you are a carbon particle. Describe your adventures. Use the diagram above to start you off. The sentences on Cut Out LW5 (Part 2) will help. Present your adventure as a play, poster or on a tape to explain the carbon cycle to a younger brother or sister.

How is nitrogen recycled?

The protein you eat is made from nitrates that were once in the soil. Page 1.7 shows more about this.

EXPLORE

There are three ways that nitrogen gets into the soil.

Nitrogen is sent around in a cycle from plants and animals, soil and air.

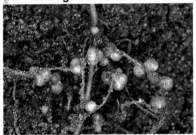

Some nitrogen-fixing bacteria between soil particles change nitrogen in the air spaces to nitrates.

Some nitrogen-fixing bacteria living in root nodules take nitrogen from the air spaces and change it into nitrates for the plants.

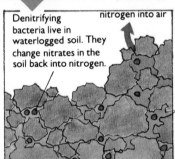

Denitrifying bacteria live in waterlogged soil. They change nitrates in the soil back into nitrogen.

nitrogen into air

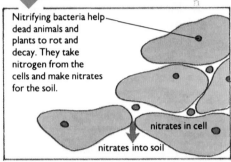

Nitrifying bacteria help dead animals and plants to rot and decay. They take nitrogen from the cells and make nitrates for the soil.

nitrates in cell

nitrates into soil

- Make a diagram to show how the nitrogen gets from one part of the cycle to another. Cut Out LW6 will help.
- **Classify** the microbes into those that add nitrogen to the soil and those that take nitrogen out of the soil.
  Record this information in a table.

What did you spray?

Farmer Giles is considering spraying chemicals on his crops to kill insects that eat the crops. Amy and Ben were discussing this. These were their **hypotheses**.

EXPLORE

- Which **hypotheses** do you agree with? What other effects do you think chemicals might have?
- If Ben's **hypotheses** are correct, mark on your cut out which part(s) of the nitrogen cycle won't work any more.
  Will plants still grow when the chemicals have been added? You are **applying**.

I think chemicals are a good idea because they kill things like maggots so that we can eat nicer food.

But bacteria are living things as well. I think they will be killed by the chemicals, too.

And the food's cheaper because it doesn't get ruined by the pests and have to be thrown away.

But I think that some of the chemicals stay in the plant so we eat those as well!

Amy

Ben

GROWING MICROBES

Where do they come from?

All around you, in the air you breathe and the soil you walk on, are tiny organisms that can only be seen with a microscope. They are called **microbes**, and include bacteria, viruses and other microscopic organisms. Four hundred years ago no one had heard of microbes. They weren't even sure where organisms they could see came from.

EXPLORE

- Make a list of the **observations** made here. Are there any that you disagree with, or would like to check?
- Make a list of the **inferences** made. Are there any that you disagree with?
- How could you test these inferences?

Urgh! This meat has gone rotten and it's full of maggots. There weren't any maggots when I put it away or I wouldn't have bothered to save it.

The maggots have been created by the meat rotting.

Look at this wheat. It's full of mice. There weren't any mice when I put it in here.

The mice have been created in the wheat.

Something from nothing?

The idea that organisms could be created out of nothing was commonly accepted until 300 years ago. Then some experimenting began!

EXPLORE

- Describe this **experiment** in your own words.
- What were the results of the experiment?
- What **interpretation** did Redi make of these results? Do you agree with it?

So, after 1668 people agreed that visible organisms were not created out of nothing. But what about microbes? Even if a jar of meat is covered it will decay because of bacteria in it. Can bacteria be created out of nothing?

- What was Spallanzani's **prediction**?
- How did he test his prediction?
- What were the results of his **experiment**?
- What **interpretation** did Spallanzani make of these results? Do you agree with it?

Not everyone was convinced by Spallanzani's experiment. People argued that air was necessary for life. They thought shutting off the air supply to the boiled food stopped more microbes being created.

- Do you think Spallanzani's experiment is a fair test?

1668 — Hi! I'm Francesco Redi, and I'm going to do an experiment to test whether rotting meat creates maggots.

There! Only the open jar has got maggots. Flies can only get to the meat in the open jars. They lay eggs which are too small to see and that's where the maggots come from. If the meat had created the maggots there would have been maggots in both jars.

1765 — Hi! I'm Lazzaro Spallanzani. I predict that food won't go bad if you kill the microbes in it. I shall kill any microbes simply by boiling them.

UNBOILED

BOILED

There! The open jar has gone bad - it smells horrible. The boiled food is still alright. By the way, I put a seal on the boiled jar to stop any more microbes getting in.

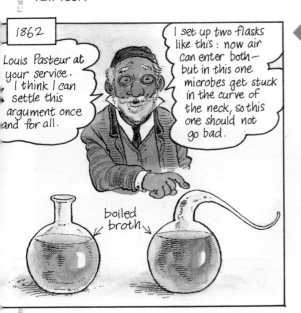

1862

Louis Pasteur at your service. I think I can settle this argument once and for all.

I set up two flasks like this: now air can enter both—but in this one microbes get stuck in the curve of the neck, so this one should not go bad.

boiled broth

Pasteur's results were just as he **predicted**. Since then most people have agreed that you cannot create living things out of non-living things.

- What did Pasteur **predict** would happen?
- Why is this experiment an improvement on Spallanzani's?
- Do you agree with the **interpretation**? Is there another explanation that would fit these results?

HARE TODAY, GONE TOMORROW

Some animals eat grass or other plants. They are called
herbivores. Some animals eat other animals. They are called
carnivores. Carnivores have to catch or hunt their food. Do you
eat other animals? If so, do you have to hunt them in the same
way? Why?

Look at the two animals below: one of them exists by eating the
other. Which do you think is the hunter and which is the
hunted? You will have to **observe** the pictures and make
inferences.

EXPLORE

■ Make a list of *similarities* you can **observe** between the two
  animals.
■ Make a list of *differences* you can **observe** between them.

The two animals have different ways of life. One needs to be a
good hunter, the other has to be able to escape from the hunter.

■ For each difference in your list, write down how you think
  the difference helps the animal to hunt or to escape.

Canadian Lynx

Snowshoe Hare

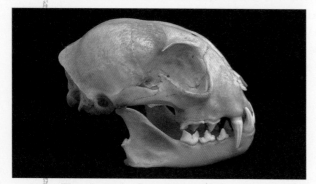
The skull of a Canadian Lynx

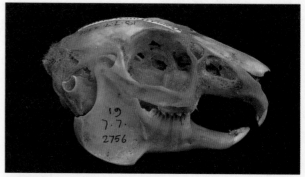
The skull of a Snowshoe Hare

1.10

Predators and prey

An animal that hunts is called a **predator**. The animal that it hunts is called its **prey**. The number of predators depends on the number of prey. If there are lots of prey, there will be lots of predators. If there are only a few prey, there will not be so many predators. Why do you think this is?

The graph shows the number of hares and lynx in one area of Canada.

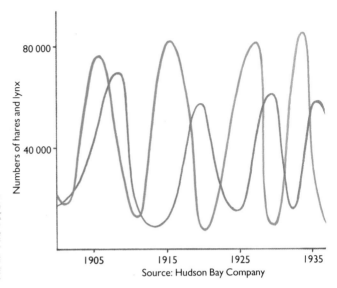

Source: Hudson Bay Company

EXPLORE

- Which line on the graph do you think shows the number of hares?
- Which line shows the number of lynx?
- Why do you think these records were kept?

PRESENT

- A biologist has been studying the populations of hares and lynx in Canada. Use Cut Out LW7 to write a page from a biologist's report explaining how the populations change.

Pierre and Virginia were looking at this diagram.

'The number of foxes is never as great as the number of rabbits', Pierre **observed**.

'Well', said Virginia 'if there were more foxes they wouldn't have enough rabbits to catch. There must always be more prey than predators.'

'Come off it , what if there were lots of small predators?', **questioned** Pierre.

'Well you could take the mass of prey and predators into account, as in this diagram for foxes and rabbits. The predators will always need a bigger mass of prey to live on', **hypothesised** Virginia.

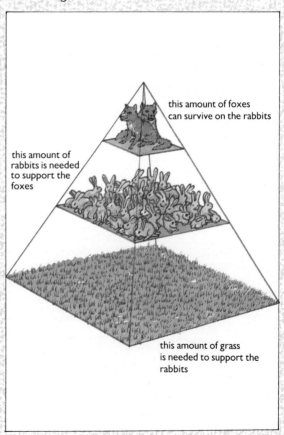

this amount of foxes can survive on the rabbits

this amount of rabbits is needed to support the foxes

this amount of grass is needed to support the rabbits

- Draw a similar pyramid for grass, hares and lynx to finish off the report.

Now look back at the title. As a way of tying these ideas together, isn't it one of the worst lynx ever?

HEART AND FITNESS

EXPLORE

- Do you agree with Dr Blob's idea?
- What 'risks' do unfit people face?
- What do you think fitness means?
- Who's the fittest person you know? What makes them fit? Are you fit?

Katy's group collected information about health and fitness for a project. They found that the average number of cigarettes smoked each day increased between 1920 and 1960. The number of deaths from lung cancer also increased between 1920 and 1960. They also found these graphs.

- **Interpret** the information shown in the diagrams using Cut Out LW8 (Part 1) to help you.

Heart Shock!

A survey published today revealed that too many of us have **high heart rates** and **high blood pressure**. Dr Blob said she was shocked. "I think that all schools and workplaces should start the day with 30 minutes of exercise. This will help people at risk to reduce their heart rate or blood pressure."

By measuring heart rate during *and* after a five-minute run you can find out your recovery time

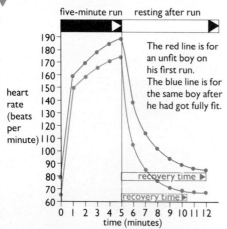

The red line is for an unfit boy on his first run.
The blue line is for the same boy after he had got fully fit.

This pie chart shows causes of death in Britain

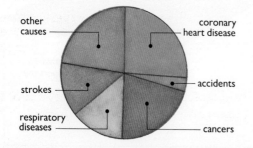

After many adults reduced the fat in their diet the numbers of deaths due to heart attacks started to fall

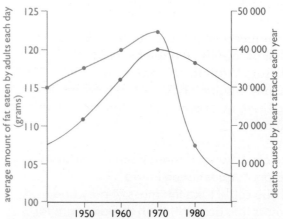

Years stopped smoking	2	6	10	15	20
Deaths per 10 000 men	10	5	3	2	2

Men who stopped smoking were less likely to die as time went on

Circulating well

Why are the heart, blood and circulation so important? Every part of the body needs a blood supply. The blood gives each organ the substances it needs and takes away any waste substances. These diagrams explain how:

EXPLORE

- **Interpret** the information and diagrams to make a table showing the differences between arteries and veins.
  You are **classifying** your **observations**.

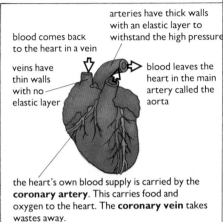

blood comes back to the heart in a vein

veins have thin walls with no elastic layer

arteries have thick walls with an elastic layer to withstand the high pressure

blood leaves the heart in the main artery called the aorta

the heart's own blood supply is carried by the **coronary artery**. This carries food and oxygen to the heart. The **coronary vein** takes wastes away.

The heart from the outside

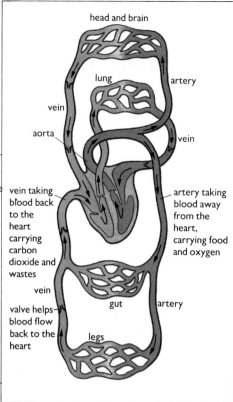

head and brain

lung

artery

vein

aorta

vein

vein taking blood back to the heart carrying carbon dioxide and wastes

artery taking blood away from the heart, carrying food and oxygen

vein

valve helps blood flow back to the heart

gut

artery

legs

How the heart circulates blood around the body

Circulating problems

There are lots of places in the heart and circulation system where things can go wrong. You have probably heard of people having high blood pressure, thrombosis, angina and heart attacks. The photos show some examples.

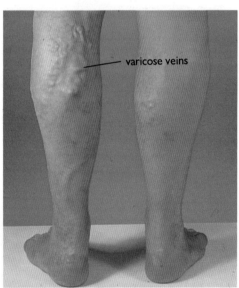

varicose veins

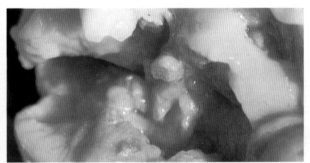

If you eat too much fatty food, cholesterol gets stuck to the side of the artery. The photograph is taken inside a completely blocked artery.

The valves swell and get painful if you spend a lot of time standing up or don't get enough exercise

PRESENT

- Make a poster for a doctor's surgery to show the things that can go wrong with people's heart and circulation. Use Cut Out LW8 (Part 2) to help.

- Add a plan of action to improve people's health and fitness. Follow your plan!

KIDS

When you were a baby you needed certain things to make you feel well, happy, safe and to help you grow and develop. Can you think of some of those needs? Do you still need things in the same way?

In the diagram are some needs of young children.
Some are things children need to keep them physically well. These are called **physical needs**. Others are things they need to keep them happy and to help them learn easily. These are called their **emotional needs**.

EXPLORE

- Complete this table for each of the needs listed in the diagram. You are **classifying**.
- Make a list of the ways you might meet these needs.

Physical needs	Emotional needs	Both needs

- Your next-door neighbour has asked you to look after his 18-month-old baby girl for 24 hours. Plan a day for the child. Make a list of all her physical needs and emotional needs. Think of all the things you would do with her to meet her needs. Check with a parent to see if he or she agrees with your plan.

Looking after children

EXPLORE

- Who do you think are the best people to look after children?
- Should mothers go out to work and let fathers look after children?
- Does it hurt children to have a variety of people looking after them?

PRESENT

- The marketing manager of a nappy company wants to know who looks after young children. Make a survey for her. Use some parents you know. Ask them who looks after their children and why they make this arrangement. Present your findings in a poster.

LEAVES

Horse chestnut

Ash

Common oak   **Beech**

Seeing is beleaving(!)

Do you try and identify the trees you see when you go for a walk? One of the easiest ways of recognising trees is by their leaves.

EXPLORE

- Look at the trees in your area. Can you find all four types of tree? Make a note of where they are.
- Which is the most common type of tree in your area?
- Collect some leaves from one type of tree. Are they all the same size? Why?

PRESENT

- Your local park keeper wants a record of which trees grow in the park, and where. Make a map for the park keeper to put on the wall.

Leaving food

To live and grow, plants need food just like you do. But they do not eat like you do – they make their own food. They do this in their leaves. The food they make is sugar, and they make it out of carbon dioxide from the air and water from the soil. To do this they need energy, which comes from sunlight. The process is called **photosynthesis**. It produces oxygen as well as sugar.

$$\text{carbon dioxide} + \text{water} \xrightarrow{\text{sunlight}} \text{sugar} + \text{oxygen}$$

Why are leaves green?

Plants use sunlight energy to photosynthesise. This is where the green colour comes in. Leaves contain a green substance called **chlorophyll** which traps sunlight energy. Chlorophyll is contained in granules called **chloroplasts** in the leaf cells. Leaves can only make sugar in sunlight. Plants need food all the time, so they store the sugar. To do this they convert it into starch which is kept as grains in the leaf cells. Why do you think they convert the sugar to starch?

Inside leaves

This diagram shows the different cells inside a leaf.

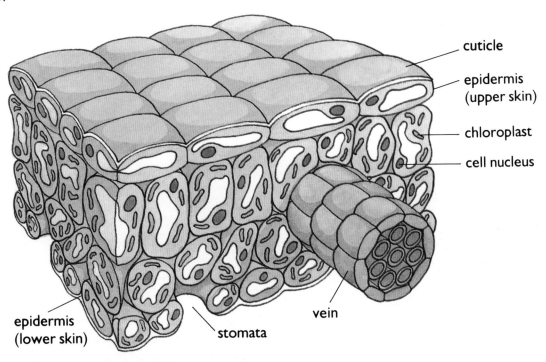

cuticle

epidermis (upper skin)

chloroplast

cell nucleus

vein

epidermis (lower skin)

stomata

EXPLORE

The cells in a leaf are organised to do different jobs. Match each kind of cells with these jobs. Use Cut Out LW9 to help you.

- these cells have lots of air space around them as they obtain carbon dioxide from the air. They also release oxygen.
- these cells are full of green chloroplasts to trap sunlight.
- these cells protect the leaf and stop it losing water.
- these cells have a number of openings to let water in and out.

PRESENT

Design a 'leaflet'(!) about the structure and function of a leaf.

PLANT GROWTH

As well as food, you need vitamins and minerals to grow and stay healthy. Do plants need them too?
Look at this photograph. These plants have all been grown from the same batch of seeds, at the same time and in the same place. The only difference is in the solutions they are growing in.

COMPLETE | −N | −P | −K | −Ca | −Mg | −S | −Fe

EXPLORE

- What variables have been controlled here, by always being the same?
- Which is the dependent variable (the one that is changed)?
- What are the independent variables (the things which change because of the investigation)?

Key
- **N** without nitrogen
- **P** without phosphorus
- **K** without potassium
- **Ca** without calcium
- **Mg** without magnesium
- **S** without sulphur
- **Fe** without iron

EXPLORE

■ Which of these **observations** go with which plants?

- The stem of this plant has only grown to about half the height of a healthy plant, but there is a greater growth of roots.

- The stem of this plant has grown to about half the size of a healthy plant, but there are very few leaves and the top ones have become yellow and shrivelled.

- The stem of this plant has only grown to a quarter of the height of a healthy plant and there is very little root growth.

- This plant has grown healthily.

- This plant has grown to about half the size of a healthy plant.

- This plant has grown to about three-quarters the size of a healthy plant but the leaves have yellow patches and the lower ones are drooping.

- This plant has not grown at all.

- This plant has only grown to about half the size of a healthy plant and the leaves are small with black patches.

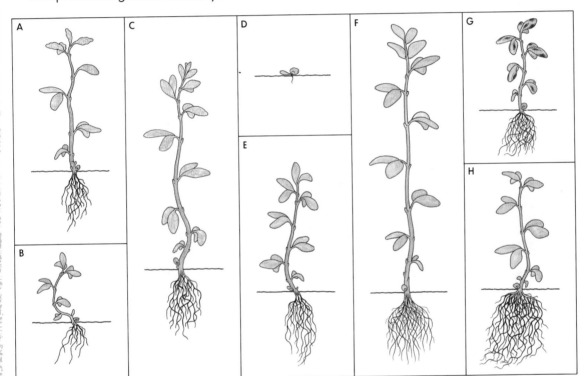

■ These drawings were made to show the important features shown by each plant. Which drawing do you think goes with which plant?

EXPLORE

■ How would you set up an investigation like this?

PRESENT

Imagine you are the person who did this experiment. Write a report.

■ Make a record of drawings and observations.

■ Write down what you think this **investigation** shows about minerals and plant growth. You are **interpreting**.

RAINFORESTS

Water evaporating helps to form rain clouds

Trees take in carbon dioxide from the air.

Trees give out oxygen.

Some plant extracts make valuable medicines.

The roots absorb rainwater.

The roots hold the soil in place and stop soil erosion.

◀ **The living rainforest is useful in many ways**

Trees of life

There are large areas of forests in tropical places where it is hot and humid. They are called **rainforests**. One country which has rainforests is Bangladesh in Asia.

EXPLORE

Discuss these questions in a small group.
- Which trees do you know of that grow in tropical rainforests?
- Which other countries have tropical rainforests?
- Think of all the ways that living trees are useful. Use the ideas in the picture to start you off. Divide your ideas into 'benefits to the environment' and 'benefits to humans'. You are **classifying** your ideas.
- If there were no trees or other plants in the world, we would all die. Why?

Cutting it down

Deforestation happens when large areas of forest are destroyed or cut down. Some people believe that floods in Bangladesh in 1988 were caused by deforestation in the area.

Faizal Ali's group were discussing what would happen if all the trees in an area like the one above were chopped down. Do you agree with them?

The tree roots won't absorb the water so it will go into rivers or streams.

If there's heavy rain in might wash the soil away.

The wood could be sold. It would provide money for local people.

You wouldn't be able to make any good local medicines.

PRESENT
- The Rainforest Appeal are launching a publicity campaign to show people the effects of deforestation. Make a poster for them. Use Cut Out LW10 (Part 1) to help you.

Brazilian rainforests

Brazil is a country in South America with large rainforests that cover about half its land. Many people live in the forests. They get their food and clothing and build their homes from plants and animals in the forest. This way of life is very important to them. They don't need anything from the outside world.

EXPLORE

- What sort of food do you think the forest people eat?
- How do you think they make their clothes and build their homes?
- How do you think they will live if the rainforest is cut down?

Everything these people need is provided by the rainforest. They are tying up wild honey in leaves and have caught an armadillo to cook ▼

The Perfect Solution?

January 1987

The population in Brazil is increasing rapidly. Many people are poor or unemployed. The Brazilian government plans to clear huge areas of rainforest to build roads, towns, mines and dams. The mines will extract the valuable minerals found under the rainforests. Valleys will be dammed and flooded for a hydroelectric power station. It is hoped that these developments will provide jobs and wealth and will attract new industries and businesses.

The World Bank, the European Community and Japan will lend money to Brazil. In return, Brazil will sell iron ore to Japan and the European Community at very cheap prices. Brazil will have to export minerals such as iron ore, wood and agricultural products to repay the loan, but after that the exports will be sold to earn money for the country.

The plan is to make Brazil wealthy and provide jobs for the people. It also means the forest people will lose their homes, because the forest valleys will be dammed and flooded.

- Make a table to show the advantages and disadvantages of the scheme in the article above. Use Cut Out LW10 (Part 2) to help you. You are **interpreting** and **inferring**.

Advantages	Disadvantages

- This project went ahead in 1987. **Apply** what you have learnt to **predict** what happened.
- Faizal Ali's group found that another rainforest was going to be chopped down to clear an area for beef cattle to supply a beefburger chain. Do you think their ideas are useful?

PRESENT

- What do you think you can do to help save the rainforest? Make a tape recording for a radio programme telling people your ideas.

My dad said we were going to get mahogany kitchen units. I think it would be better to get a fast-growing wood like pine.

I think I'm going to join a group that cares about rainforests.

We could write and complain. Who shall we write to...?

RECYCLING

What a load of rubbish

Many things that we throw away can be recycled and used again. What advantages do you think this has?

PRESENT

Your local council is producing a leaflet telling people what's in the rubbish they collect. They want an eyecatching diagram.

- Draw a bar chart to show what our rubbish is made up of.
- In each bar list the things that you throw away that are made of this material.
- Paper, metals, glass and organic matter are easy to recycle. This means they be used again. What percentage (%) is this? Show it on your bar chart.

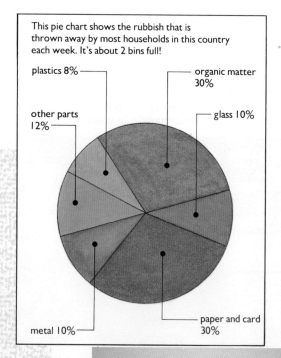

This pie chart shows the rubbish that is thrown away by most households in this country each week. It's about 2 bins full!

plastics 8%

organic matter 30%

other parts 12%

glass 10%

metal 10%

paper and card 30%

Case Study 1: Making new paper

Logs are cut into small chips, then heated with various chemicals to make wood pulp. This is bleached to make white paper like the paper used to make this book. Chemicals and bleach cause serious pollution to rivers and lakes if they are not disposed of carefully.

This is how paper is recycled ▶

Trees are chopped down to make pap

EXPLORE

- List all the things you use that are made of paper. Are any of them made of recycled paper?
- Put a tick next to the ones that you wouldn't mind using recycled paper for.
- Do you think recycled paper should be used more? If so, what could you do to encourage people to use more recycled paper?
- Make a table to show the advantages and disadvantages of using recycled paper.

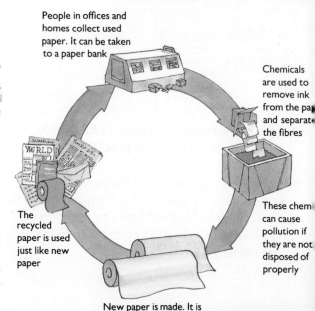

People in offices and homes collect used paper. It can be taken to a paper bank

Chemicals are used to remove ink from the pap and separat the fibres

These chem can cause pollution if they are not disposed of properly

The recycled paper is used just like new paper

New paper is made. It is off-white in colour because it has not been bleached

Case Study 2: Producing aluminium

Aluminium comes from an ore called bauxite. Bauxite is often found under forests or agricultural land. A mine and a power station must be built to get the ore out of the ground. What effect do you think this has on the local environment?

Expensive electrical energy is needed to get aluminium (front) from bauxite (back)

EXPLORE

- List the advantages and disadvantages of recycling aluminium.
- Draw diagrams to show how glass and organic matter are recycled. Use Cut Out LW11 (Part 1) to help you.
- Complete the summary chart on Cut Out LW11 (Part 2) about recycling. You are **interpreting**.

This is how aluminium is recycled

The cans are melted. This uses less energy than producing new aluminium

People put cans in skips like this

These new cans are used. About 50% of aluminium is recycled in this country

New cans are made using far less energy and money and producing less pollution

A smaller load of rubbish?

As well as saving money and resources, recycling reduces the amount of waste we produce. Ella's group were discussing this at the bottle bank.

EXPLORE

- Which ideas do you agree with? What other ideas do you have to encourage recycling?
- Which ideas do you think could work in your area?

PRESENT

- Write a letter to your MP saying what you want done in your area to encourage recycling. You are **applying** what you've learnt.

> This one's got a deposit on it. We'd better take it back to the shop.

> I don't think we should worry about pollution and energy - someone will invent something else before it's a serious problem.

> All bottles should have a deposit - it would save even more energy and raw materials than bottle banks.

> Anyway, we pay rates or poll tax - it's the council who are responsible for all this.

> There'd be less litter as well. I think aluminium cans should have a deposit system as well.

SEX DETERMINATION

Here are some ideas people have about how baby boys and girls are formed. Do you agree with any of them?

PRESENT

Your local health visitor wants to know how many boys and girls there are in your area, and what their parents think about them.

- Do a survey of some families that you know and write her a report.
- Record how many boys and how many girls are in each family.
- Ask people why they think that sometimes a baby boy is born and other times it's a baby girl.
- Ask them if it makes any difference to the family whether they have a baby boy or a baby girl.
- What other questions could you ask them? Include the answers in your report.

They're made by storks and brought to the hospital, so the stork decides the sex.

Girl babies are made if the mother is upset about something.

Baby boys are made if the father is dominant.

Baby girls are made if the parents have sex at full moon.

The baby will be a boy if the mother sleeps on her back the night it's conceived.

Here are some other ideas about how you get a baby girl or a baby boy.

A baby gets some of its characteristics from its mother's egg...

... and some from its father's sperm.

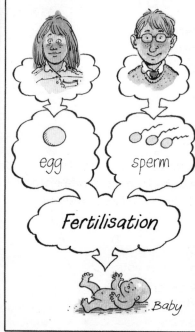

egg

sperm

Fertilisation

Baby

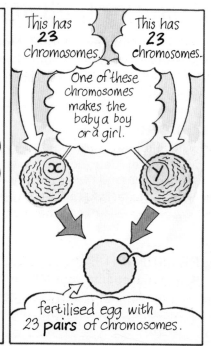

This has **23** chromosomes.

This has **23** chromosomes.

One of these chromosomes makes the baby a boy or a girl.

fertilised egg with 23 **pairs** of chromosomes.

Chromosomes are thread-like structures found in all cells. They carry information. The chromosomes in your mother's egg and father's sperm decide your characteristics like your sex, eye colour and hair type.

These photos show the sex chromosomes in the egg and the sperm.

Sex chromosomes in the egg look like an 'X'

Sperm sex chromosomes can look like either an 'X' shape or a 'Y' shape

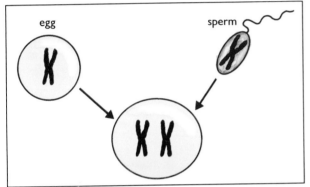

Baby girls have an X chromosome from the egg and an X chromosome from the sperm

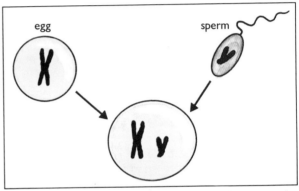

Baby boys have an X chromosome from the egg and a Y chromosome from the sperm

EXPLORE
■ How are baby boys and baby girls made? Playing the game on Cut Out LW12 will help you sort your ideas out.
■ If a man produced lots of sperm with Y sex chromosomes what sex would his baby probably be?
■ What sort of sperm is needed to make a baby girl?

PRESENT
■ Make a poster for your local family planning clinic showing how boy and girl babies are formed. Use your own ideas and those from your survey.

Knowing in advance

Pregnant women often go to the doctor for check-ups. The doctor can do tests to see if both the baby and the mother are all right. One of the tests they can do tells the sex of the baby.

EXPLORE
■ Would you like to know the sex of your baby before it is born?
■ Would it matter if it was a baby girl or a baby boy?

SICKLE-CELL ANAEMIA

We all need oxygen to run, jump, swim and even sleep. The oxygen we breathe in is carried from the lungs to all our body cells by the blood. In fact it's carried by **haemoglobin** in red blood cells.

Blood carries oxygen around the body.

Anaemic people look really pale.

I think haemoglobin makes blood red.

I know iron tablets come into this somewhere.

EXPLORE

- What is the most important job the blood does?
- What do people mean when they say they're anaemic? Here are some ideas to start you off.

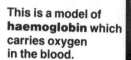

This is a model of **haemoglobin** which carries oxygen in the blood.

- Look at the two photos of red blood cells. What differences can you **observe**?
- How active do you think the people who gave these blood samples are? You are **inferring**.

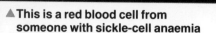

▲ This is a red blood cell from someone with sickle-cell anaemia

◄ These are red blood cells from someone who doesn't have anaemia

The blood sample on the right is from a person with **sickle-cell anaemia**. The red cells have collapsed and formed an S-shape like a sickle. [A sickle is a tool with a semi-circular blade used for cutting long grass.]

Sickle-cell anaemia is caused by a special form of haemoglobin. People who have this type of haemoglobin inherit it from their parents. It is an example of an **inherited disease**.

How do people inherit sickle-cell haemoglobin?

A baby inherits half its chromosomes from its mother and half from its father. Each chromosome is made up of many genes. One particular gene controls how the body makes haemoglobin. A baby gets *one* haemoglobin gene from its mother and *one* from its father.

In this case, the baby inherits two round-shaped haemoglobin genes. It will produce round-shaped haemoglobin.

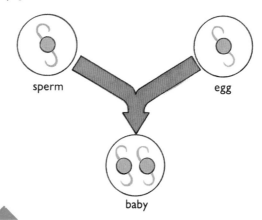

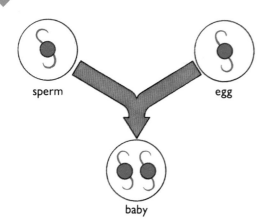

In this case, the baby inherits two sickle-cell haemoglobin genes. All the red blood cells it produces will be sickle shaped. They will not carry oxygen very well and the baby will suffer from anaemia and may die.

In this case, the baby inherits one sickle-cell gene and one round-shaped gene. The blood cells only collapse under very unusual circumstances, so the baby is as healthy as one with two round-shaped genes. In fact the baby has an advantage, because it cannot catch malaria—the microbe that causes malaria feeds on round-shaped haemoglobin, but cannot digest sickle-cell haemoglobin.

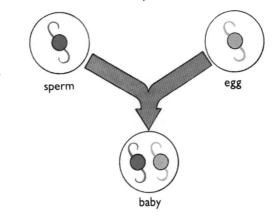

EXPLORE

- Can a baby inherit sickle-cell anaemia if both its parents have two round-shaped haemoglobin genes?
- Where would it be an advantage to have one sickle-cell gene and one round-shaped one?
- Sickle-cell anaemia is a particular kind of anaemia. Find out about one other kind and how it can be cured.

PRESENT

A doctor has been sent to a part of the USA to investigate reports of an unknown disease. She suspects that the disease, which affects digestion, may be inherited, as it has only been reported in a few families who live in remote areas. Local people think that the disease may be caused by the strange diet of the families.

- Write an account of the doctor's investigations.

TAKING RESPONSIBILITY

Just good friends

When people start to mature they may have relationships with other people. There are lots of things to learn about the other person when you have a relationship. Having sex can be part of that relationship, but it doesn't have to be. If you do have sex it is extremely important to be responsible about it and to really get to know the other person first.

EXPLORE

- What important things do you look for in your friends?
- Why do you think friends are so important?
- How can you tell when someone is not being a good friend to you?

The Harry and Anita story . . .

EXPLORE

- What do you think are the most important things to look for in a loving relationship?
- Do you think Harry and Anita should get together?
- Finish the story the way you think things should turn out.

Being responsible about sex

As you get older you will probably have some good friends. Sometimes you will form loving relationships with other people. In these relationships you might have sex. Not everyone agrees about how old you should be when you have sex, or with whom you should have it.

Here are some people's ideas and attitudes to having sex.

You should only have sex when you're married and only to have children.

You should only have sex when the other person says they love you.

It doesn't matter when you have sex as long as you use a contraceptive.

Only have sex when you really love and trust the other person.

You should only have sex when you're married.

You can have sex any time as long as it doesn't get heavy.

You should only have sex when you're really committed to each other.

I have sex whenever I can as long as I'm not hurting anyone.

You should only have sex when you're really sure you both want to and are ready.

It's important to have lots of different sexual experiences before you get married.

Boys can have sex anytime but girls shouldn't because they'll get a bad name.

You should only have sex with someone you really like.

EXPLORE
- Which ideas do you most agree with?
- What things other than sex do you think are important in a loving relationship?
- How would you define having a responsible attitude to sex?

PRESENT
- Make up a radio discussion in a group of four about having a responsible attitude to sex.

VARIATION IN LIVING THINGS

EXPLORE

- Why do you think children in one family are different, although they had the same parents?
- Do children ever look exactly the same? Why do you think this happens?

You must be kitting

Sally and Toby's cat had kittens.
'They're different', **observed** Toby.
'That's because each kitten comes from a different egg from the mother and sperm from the father', **interpreted** Sally. 'They all have different genes.'
'They're all the same size though', said Toby.
'Does that mean they will stay the same size all their life?'
'No, they're bound to get bigger as they get older', replied Sally.
'I don't mean that', said Toby. 'As they get bigger, will they all be the same size? Will they get bigger at the same rate?' Sally and Toby gave the kittens away to friends, but they weighed five of them every month to see if they could answer Toby's **question**. Here are the figures they collected.

EXPLORE

- Draw a line graph of these results. Use a different colour line for each kitten.
- Do you agree with Sally's and Toby's ideas?
- How could you improve on this **investigation**?

Mass after

Kitten	1 Month	2 Months	3 Months	4 Months	5 Months
Annabel	250g	300g	350g	370g	390g
Basil	240g	310g	400g	460g	520g
Claws	250g	270g	280g	270g	280g
Dixon	260g	300g	340g	380g	420g
Ermintrude	280g	350g	420g	440g	430g

Sally and Toby **evaluated** these results.
'They've all got bigger at different rates', **interpreted** Sally.
'I suppose that's what you'd expect', said Toby. 'After all they've all had different things to eat and lived in different places.'
'Yes', agreed Sally. 'The people who had Annabel gave her fish every day.'
'And Claws got lost for three days', said Toby.
'All these things must make a difference to cats—or any living things', said Sally.

Don't bug me

A new insect has been discovered. It's name is *Atphor levphor*,
but it is known as the SiP bug for short.
These drawings were made of a small population of SiP bugs.

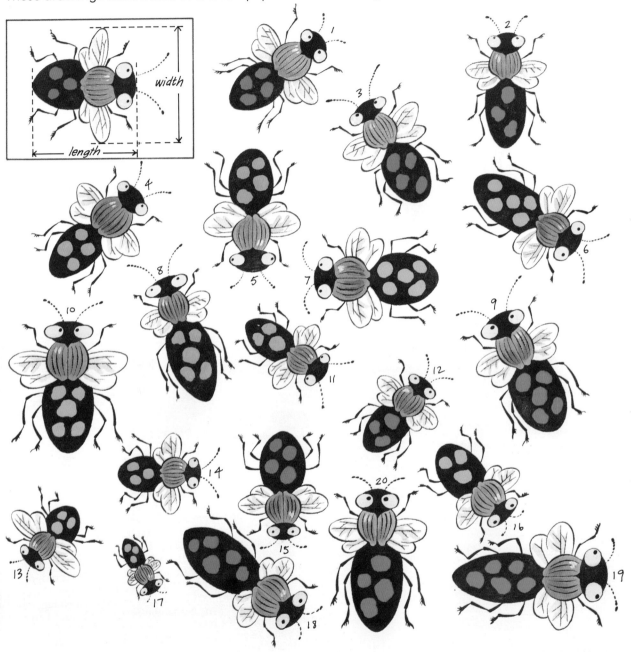

EXPLORE
- What **characteristics** (features) of the bugs do not vary?
- What characteristics of the bugs show a **range** of variation?

PRESENT
- Measure and record the variable characteristics you have found. Present your figures as a wall chart to help you give a lecture about this new discovery. Add bar charts to show the amount of variation in each characteristic.

VIRUSES AND BACTERIA

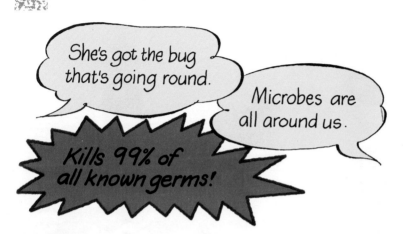

She's got the bug that's going round.

Microbes are all around us.

Kills 99% of all known germs!

Don't bug me

EXPLORE
- Here are some examples of people using the words 'bugs', 'germs' and 'microbes'. Think of some more ways people use these words.
- What do you think the words mean?

What are bugs?

People usually mean **bacteria** or **viruses** when they talk about bugs, germs and microbes. These articles tell us more about bacteria and viruses.

FOOD SCARE!

Forty cases of food poisoning were reported yesterday. Tests showed that salmonella bacteria in chicken pâté was the cause.

Dr Bird explained why there have been so many outbreaks recently.

Salmonella bacterium

'All bacteria are living things made of only one cell with a nucleus. They can only be seen with a microscope so you can't see the bacteria when you buy food.

'If it's warm and moist, like inside the human body, bacteria reproduce and grow rapidly. They divide into two every 20 minutes, so one bacterium can produce millions in a short time!'

Salmonella bacteria make poisons called toxins, but some bacteria harm humans by destroying body cells.

▲ HIV viruses (Shown orange)

HIV VIRUS AND AIDS. . .

The number of people infected with the HIV virus has increased. Viruses are smaller than bacteria so a powerful microscope is needed to see them.

Like all viruses, the HIV virus has no nucleus and it cannot feed, grow, move or respire. It can only reproduce. It does this inside the cells of living things such as humans. One virus invades a cell and lots of viruses can emerge to infect other cells. This harms the person and spreads the disease through the body.

In some people the HIV virus takes over the body, and the disease called AIDS can develop.

EXPLORE
- Make a table using these headings to compare the HIV virus with salmonella bacteria. Underline the points that apply to all bacteria and viruses. You are **interpreting**. Add any other things that your group knows about bacteria and viruses.

	Bacteria	Viruses
Size		
How do they reproduce?		
What conditions do they like?		

Good and bad

Salmonella and HIV can be harmful to humans, but some microbes are useful. Find out more about microbes. Use the information cards on Cut Out LW13 to help you.

The body's defence against disease

You have **white blood cells** in your blood to fight any microbes that enter your body.

EXPLORE

- List any diseases that you think you have **acquired immunity** for.
- Immunity can also be given by an injection called a **vaccination**. List the diseases you have been vaccinated against.
- What diseases in other parts of the world can people be vaccinated against? (Use the information cards on Cut Out LW13 to help you.)

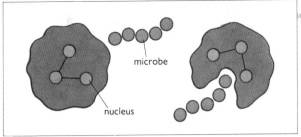

One type of white blood cell can 'eat' any microbes that it meets

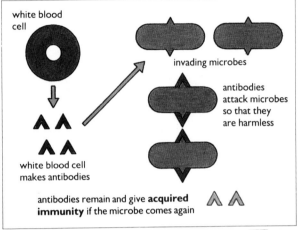

Another type of white blood cell produces chemicals called **antibodies** to fight the microbes

Using drugs to fight disease

If your body can't get rid of a disease on its own, the doctor might give you drugs called **antibiotics**. Penicillin was one of the first antibiotics—it was discovered by mistake!

EXPLORE

- **Record** which of Fleming's statements is an **observation**, an **inference**, a **hypothesis** or a **prediction**.
- Have you ever had penicillin? If so, what illness was it for?
- Some people can't take penicillin. Why not?

PRESENT

- The school nurse was going to give a lesson about preventing disease but she fell ill!
  Prepare a talk with pictures to show people all the things they can do to avoid being ill.

YOUNG THINGS

People have babies, horses have foals and swans have cygnets. Plants produce other new plants too—in fact all living things **reproduce**. What do you think would happen if they didn't?

Why have babies?

Here are some ideas about why people might want to reproduce.

EXPLORE

- Which ideas seem good reasons to you?
- Which reasons do you disagree with?
- Add some reasons of your own.

Different organisms reproduce in different ways. Dandelions produce seeds and birds lay eggs. Some animals, including humans produce eggs inside the female's body which are **fertilised** there (they are joined by a sperm from the male to start a baby).

It proves you're a real man.

I need a son to build railways and play football with.

I like cuddling little children.

We like having sex. It didn't happen on purpose.

It's an instinct—nature's way of carrying on the species.

Other people would think there was something wrong if we didn't have children.

I just love children.

We thought it would help our relationship.

We must carry on the family name.

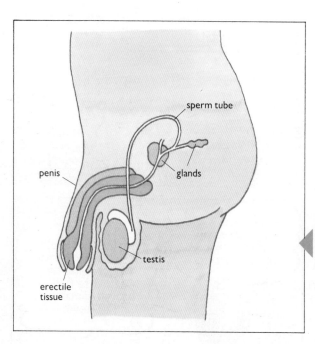

How it's done

Here is the part of a man which is designed for fertilisation. The **testes** make the sex cells called **sperm**. The sperm is carried from the testes to the penis in the sperm tubes. Before sexual intercourse the penis becomes filled with blood which makes it stiff and erect. As the sperm travels down the sperm tube a liquid called **semen** is added to the sperm. The semen is released through the opening in the penis.

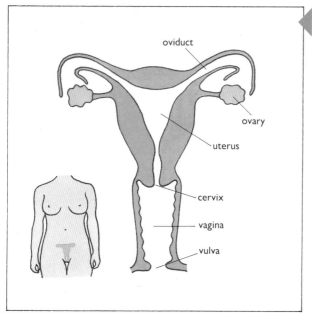

Here is the part of a woman which is designed for making eggs and producing babies. There are two **ovaries** which make the eggs. Each month one ovary releases an egg into an oviduct. Here it can be fertilised by a sperm. If it is, the fertilised egg travels down the oviduct and starts to develop in the uterus. If the egg is not fertilised it passes out of the body through the uterus and vagina. This is what happens when girls have periods. What do you think the first sign of pregnancy might be?

EXPLORE

- Make a labelled diagram of the female and male reproductive systems showing what each part does. Cut Out LW14 (Part 1) will help. You are **interpreting**.

The crucial moment—fertilisation

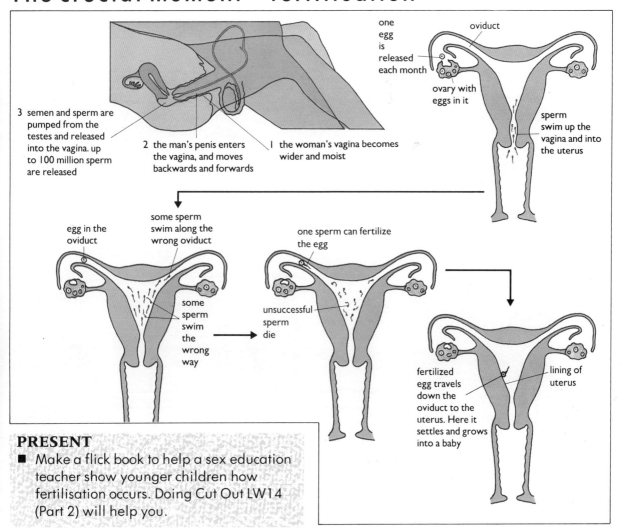

PRESENT

- Make a flick book to help a sex education teacher show younger children how fertilisation occurs. Doing Cut Out LW14 (Part 2) will help you.

YOUR LIFE

Do you want to live for a long time? Do you want to be happy? Do you want to be healthy? Most people do, of course. But they don't always know what to do to make it more likely.

EXPLORE

- Play 'Your life'. The aim of 'Your life' is to stay on the board as long as possible. Throw a die and move that number of squares. At a 'discuss' square, go **back 2** if your group thinks the situation is good, go **forward 2** if it's bad and stay where you are if it makes no difference. The information on Cut Out LW15 will help. At a chance square, pick up a chance card.

YOUNG ADULT

You stop taking regular exercise and start getting fat! Bad habits! GO FORWARD 2.

You start doing a course on first-aid and health care.

CHANCE

You are having a sexual relationship with your partner. You decide that you should have "safer sex".

CHANCE

You are very worried that you are too fat. You've lost about 15kg already and want to lose another 5kg. The doctor says you've got anorexia.

You get bad acne and can't help squeezing your spots and blackheads.

Adolescence

CHANCE

You take every opportunity to the Sun or to hot s to li

You find out you are colour blind. You can't tell the difference between reds and greens.

You are immunised against polio, diptheria, tetanus and whooping cough.

CHANCE

You are born in an area with a high amount of radioactivity in the air.

BIRTH! You are born with haemophilia. This means that your blood doesn't clot properly. You have to go to hospital if you cut yourself or you will die. GO FORWARD 5.

conception

START HERE!

Your mother has German measles while pregnant

Your parents go to ante-natal classes to learn about birth and childcare. GO BACK 1

Your father is smoking heavily while your mother is pregnant.

The game board contains the following spaces:

- ...HOOD
- You decide to stop smoking!
- You work in a factory with a lot of dust and a lot of noise.
- You develop stomach ulcers due to a bad diet and stress at work. GO FORWARD 1.
- CHANCE
- You have arthritis. Your finger joints are stiff, swollen and very painful.
- You have to work long hours and the job is very stressful. GO FORWARD 1
- There is high air pollution in your area.
- Your sight and hearing are poorer and your bones are very brittle.
- You move to an area with a nuclear power station nearby.
- CHANCE
- CHANCE
- A miracle cure is announced for your illness. GO BACK 2.
- OLD AGE
- CHANCE
- You have leukaemia and have a 50% chance of living. Continue the game if you throw a 4, 5 or 6. IF NOT— You DIE!
- You start jogging every day and feel years younger. GO BACK 3.
- You feel tired all the time. The homeopath gives you a remedy which you take.
- ...decide to eat ...fruit and ...ables. ...ACK
- CHANCE
- MIDDLE AGE

...PLORE

...ot everything in the game happens to everyone! Which things have happened to you?
...Which do you think could happen in the future? You are **predicting**.
...Make a table to show things that are caused by 'bacteria and viruses', 'food and diet',
...ifestyle', 'medicines' and 'other'. You are **classifying**.
...nderline in red things you can control. Underline in blue things you can't control.
...ou are **interpreting**.
...What can you do to make your life healthier? You are **applying**.

...ESENT

...ake a poster for your local health centre. Collect newspaper and magazine articles to
...how what sort of things affect people's lives. Make it clear which ones you think lead to a
...ealthy life and which to an unhealthy life.

CHEMICAL REACTIONS

What is energy?

Coal and gas are **energy sources**—they provide energy for heating, cooking and making electricity. What do you think energy *is*?

The bonfire party

Juber and Kamal were at a bonfire night celebration. They saw some beautiful fireworks.
'What a waste of energy', said Juber.
'Why? There's no energy in fireworks', replied Kamal.
'Of course there is! 'exclaimed Juber.
'How do you know?' asked Kamal.
'Well, you can see it, hear it, and smell it when it explodes.'
'But where was the energy before then?' asked Kamal.

EXPLORE

- How would you answer Kamal?
- Where do you think the energy went?

The power cut

Later that night Juber and Kamal were talking. The electricity suddenly went off.

EXPLORE

- Who do you agree with, Kamal or Juber?
- How do you think you can tell whether energy is involved in a situation? Make a list of ways.
- How could you test to see if there is energy in fireworks or candles?

Kamal's test

Kamal decided to measure how much energy candles have in them. This is what he did.

EXPLORE

 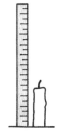 

I weighed the candle before and after the experiment.

I measured the candle before the experiment and every five minutes during the experiment.

I lit the candle and let it burn for 25 minutes.

- Did he do a fair test?
- Is this a good way of measuring energy?
- Kamal thought that the candle had 10 cm of energy at the beginning and 5 cm of energy at the end. Do you agree with his idea?
- How could you improve on his idea?

My results

Weight before:		Weight after:				
length at time: (minutes)	0	5	10	15	20	25
	10cm	9cm	8cm	7cm	6cm	5cm

Seeing the light

Kamal went back to Juber and told him about his experiment. This is what they said.

The energy just disappeared from the candle.

No it didn't. You got some heat and light, didn't you?

Yes.

Well then, the **chemical energy** in the candle was changed into **heat** and **light energy**, wasn't it?

EXPLORE
- Who do you think was right, Juber or Kamal?
- What energy do you think is involved in this photo and where does it go to? You are **applying** your ideas.
- Look back at the photo of the fireworks. What energy is involved and where does it go to?

COMPARING ROCKS AND MINERALS

Rock on, Minnie

Imagine you are walking along a wet beach with bare feet. How would the sand feel? How would it feel to stub your toe on a stone? Would you like to climb a cliff in bare feet? The Earth is made up of lots of different substances. People get valuable jewels and gold from the Earth too.

Two words are used to **classify** all these substances — **rocks** and **minerals**. The words can have different meanings depending on how you use them.

EXPLORE

- Look at the diagram and decide which word, 'rock(s)' or 'mineral(s)', would best fit each sentence.
- Think of some other meanings of the words 'rocks' and 'minerals'.
- In which situations do you think the words have a 'scientific' meaning?

This packet of milk contains lots of vitamins and _____.

This _____ water tastes the same as tap water to me.

I bought this stick of _____ while I was on holiday.

There are lots of _____ on this beach.

What are they used for?

Rocks are made up of various minerals. If we want to use a rock or mineral, we call the state we find it in the Earth the **raw material**.

Here are some examples of how rocks and minerals are used.

Marble is used for building

Diamond is used for jewellery

EXPLORE

- Write a sentence to explain why each substance is used in the way shown.

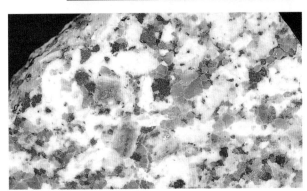

Which are they?

Here are some other useful rocks and minerals.

EXPLORE

- Match each photo to one of these names:
  - granite ● salt ● flint

  (You might need to use reference books.)
- What do you think these rocks and minerals are used for? You are **inferring**.
- What other rocks and minerals do you know? Look around your classroom for ideas.

Rocks and minerals can be **classified** in many ways, for example by age, colour, attractiveness or hardness.

PRESENT

- You are a geologist who has just 'discovered' all the rocks and minerals shown on these pages. Choose a way to **classify** them. Make a table for your report showing your groups. Add more examples you could 'discover' in each group.

EXPLORE

- Find out about the properties and uses of rocks and minerals. Use Cut Out TEB1 and photos from magazines to help you. Complete a table like this.
- Now **classify** the rocks and minerals by their uses. Name the groups you choose. Make a poster showing your classification.

Name of Rock or Mineral	Properties	Uses

PRESENT

- Jamie started to draw a picture of a kitchen to show all the ways that minerals and rocks are used. Copy it and label it for him. You are **applying** what you have learnt.

2.2

COPCOM PLC

Using copper

These photographs show some things made from copper. How do you think a pure copper lump could be made into these shapes?

EXPLORE

- Which of these ideas do you agree with?
- What other things do you know that are made of copper? What are they used for and how are they made?
- What does this tell you about the properties of copper? These are your **inferences**.

> I think a strong person uses a hammer to make those pipes.

> But I thought metals were very strong. They must have had a machine to do it.

> I'm not sure. If the metal was very strong you wouldn't be able to bend it.

> Perhaps there's another way. Maybe they use heat or pressure or something.

Object	What is it used for?	How is it made?	What property of copper does this show?
Pipes	Carrying water	It must be bent	Copper can be bent it is malleable
Saucepan	Cooking		

PRESENT

- A rich aunt has made you managing director of her copper mining company. Make a table like this to present to the board of directors showing what you can make from the copper and how.

From copper ore to copper

Before copper can be used it has to be **extracted** from the Earth by mining. A company called Copcom PLC wants to open a copper mine. They ask a mining adviser to consider two places, Exe and Wye. She has to find out about the copper ore at each place and decide which is the best place for a mine. The mining adviser found that there were different types of copper ore at Exe and Wye. She provided the photos, graphs and charts shown here and on the next page.

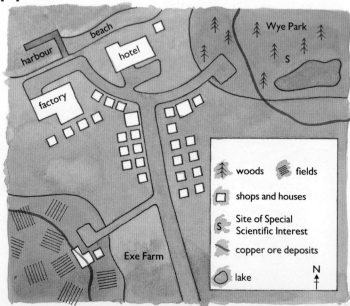

Wye Park

harbour
beach
hotel
factory
Exe Farm

woods   fields
shops and houses
S Site of Special Scientific Interest
copper ore deposits
lake

N

EXPLORE

Look at the photos of the two different copper ores.

- What are the differences between the two ores? You are **observing**.

Use all the data to answer these questions. You are **interpreting**.

- How much pure copper can be extracted from one tonne of the copper ore at Wye?
- How deep is the copper ore found at Exe?
- How much does it cost to extract copper at a depth of 200 m?
- What would be the problems of opening a mine in between Exe and Wye?
- Why do you think there is no copper ore to the west of Exe?

Copper ore from Exe

Copper ore from Wye

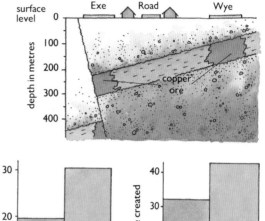

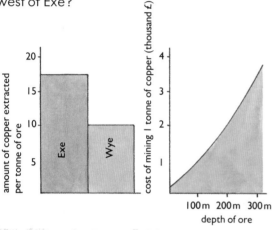

PRESENT

The mining adviser decided to present a table of information to her boss.

- Finish it for her.
- With the information so far, which site do you think is best for the mine?

  Imagine you are the mining adviser. You have to use all the information to decide if the mine should be at Exe or Wye.

- Make a list of the advantages and disadvantages for having the mine at Exe. Now do the same for Wye. For each list that you make, rank each bit of information in order of importance.
- Decide which site is best and present a report to Copcom PLC. Include advice on how the company should deal with local opposition.

	Exe	Wye
Distance from the harbour		
Type of copper ore found		
Amount of pure copper in 1 tonne of ore		

DRIFTING CONTINENTS

EXPLORE
- What things do you know about earthquakes and volcanoes?
- Where do you think they are found?

Record your ideas.

The height of disaster

Donna's group had the idea that earthquakes and volcanoes always happen near mountains. They found this map to check their idea. They also found the list on the opposite page of some large earthquakes and volcanoes.

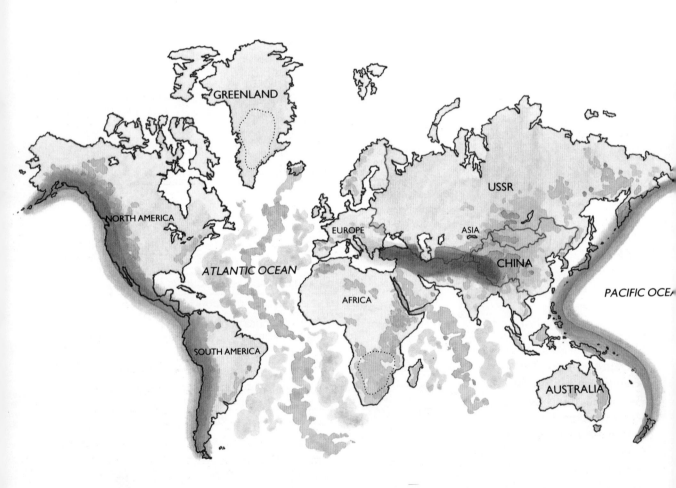

 ocean basin

 mid-ocean ridge (new rock)

 mountain range

 trench

very old rocks

EXPLORE

- Make a map showing the positions of the volcanoes and earthquakes shown on the list. Use Cut Out TEB2 (Part 1) to help you. Add others that you know of as well.
- Record any patterns that you notice. Use Cut Out TEB2 (Part 1) to help you. You are **interpreting**.

Major earthquakes	
1906 Valpariso	Chile
1908 San Francisco	USA
1923 Tokyo	Japan
1927 Nanking	China
1931 Managua	Nicaragua
1934 Northern India	
1940 Erzincan	Turkey
1988 Yerevan	USSR

Major volcanoes	
Thera (Santorini)	Greece
Surtsey	Iceland
Tristan da Cunha	Atlantic
Mt St Helens	San Francisco
Mayon	Philippines
Novarupta	East tip of USSR
North Island	New Zealand

Earth-moving ideas

Here are some ideas that people have had about why the Earth has mountains, oceans and continents in the places that it does.

Early theories

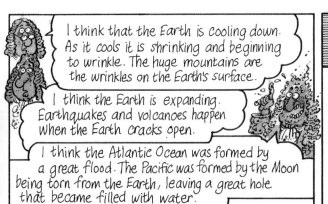

I think that the Earth is cooling down. As it cools it is shrinking and beginning to wrinkle. The huge mountains are the wrinkles on the Earth's surface.

I think the Earth is expanding. Earthquakes and volcanoes happen when the Earth cracks open.

I think the Atlantic Ocean was formed by a great flood. The Pacific was formed by the Moon being torn from the Earth, leaving a great hole that became filled with water.

Alfred Wegener

In 1915 Alfred Wegener noticed that the west coast of Africa was similar to the east coast of South America.

I think these continents were once joined together. The Atlantic Ocean formed when the two continents drifted away from each other. This is my **Continental Drift Theory**.

Most people rejected this theory. Nobody could explain why continents should start to move apart in the first place.

EXPLORE

- Write down any more ideas that you have heard.
- Read each speech bubble again, including your own ideas. Decide which are **observations, inferences** and **hypotheses**.
- Write down all the evidence there is for each theory. Use Cut Out TEB2 (Part 2) to help you.
- What do you think the arrows on the map mean? You are **applying** what you have learnt.

In the 1960s a "**mid-Atlantic ridge**" of mountains and volcanoes was discovered at the bottom of the Atlantic Ocean.

These samples show that the rocks at the top of the ridge are younger than the rocks on the ocean floor.

ocean ridge
ocean floor
molten rock

I think that molten rock from the centre of the Earth gets forced out of the cracks in the ocean floor, forming a ridge. As more rock pours out, the ocean floor starts to spread away from the ridge and slowly pushes the continents apart. This is the **Sea Floor Spreading Theory**

PRESENT

- Decide which theory you think best explains why oceans, mountains, continents, earthquakes and volcanoes are found where they are. Make a poster to convince someone from the Geological Society you are right. Include maps, diagrams and other evidence.

EARTHFORMS

Have you ever climbed a mountain? If so, were you impressed by its sheer size? You might think that large features such as mountains, oceans and rivers have always been there. In fact, they have formed slowly over millions of years. Do you think they are still changing?

Dead salty

Here is a picture of the Dead Sea. It is so salty that you can't sink in the water. It lets you float.

The Dead Sea is slowly changing. The diagrams show what scientists think will happen to the Dead Sea over the next 15 million years.

water evaporates and forms clouds

this leaves salts and dead fish

sediments are washed in by rivers

the salt is pushed up in the middle

the sediment squashes the salt

salt

EXPLORE

■ Write a sentence to describe what is happening in each picture. You are **interpreting**.

■ Draw a diagram to show how you think the Dead Sea might have formed. You are **inferring**.

more sediment squashes down on top of the salt

the salt becomes a circular dome

Earthforms formed

EXPLORE

Here are some features in the world which are a result of the process described above.

■ Match each photo to one of the stages shown above. You are **inferring**.

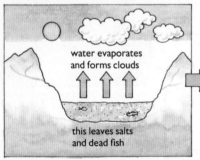

Great Salt ▲ Desert, Utah, USA

Salt dome, Bandar Abbas, Iran ▶

2.5

Tall stories

This is what the Himalayas look like today. They haven't always been like this. About 35 million years ago the rocks they are made of were layers of sediment at the bottom of the ocean. The sediments were squeezed upwards to form the mountains, and the ocean disappeared. The sediments continued to be squeezed up and the Himalayas have nearly reached their maximum height. From now on they will be **eroded** (worn away) and become flatter. Eventually (in 200 million years!) they will not exist. So the total life of the Himalayan mountains will be about 235 million years. How do you think we know all this?

Ups and downs

EXPLORE

- Copy the time line into your book. Use a whole page.
- Describe the Himalayas at each mark on the time line. Use Cut Out TEB3 to help you.
- Find photos in magazines and travel brochures which show mountains at different stages. Match each picture to one of the stages on the time line.

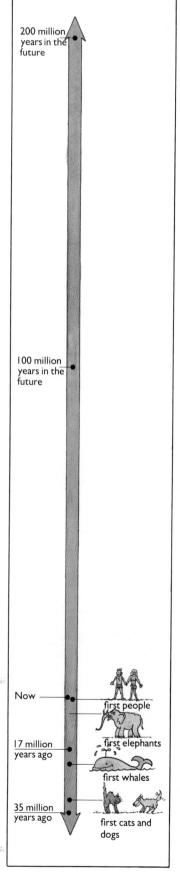

200 million years in the future

100 million years in the future

Now — first people

17 million years ago — first elephants

first whales

35 million years ago — first cats and dogs

EARTHQUAKES AND VOLCANOES

Natural disasters

What's the worst thing you can imagine happening to your community? Some natural events can have a very dramatic effect on people's lives in a very short time. The pictures show some effects of earthquakes or volcanoes.

This is Mount Etna, a volcano in Sicily

This is what happens to vineyards on the slopes when Mount Etna erupts

This is a street in San Francisco

This is the effect of an earthquake on San Francisco

EXPLORE

- Discuss what you can see in the 'before' and 'after' pictures. Use these words to start your discussion.

lava	trees
landslide	destruction
fire	fear
people	rubble

- Record what you have discussed. Make lists to compare the pictures 'before' and 'after'.
- What things do you think might have happened which are not shown in the pictures? Add these to your lists. You are **inferring**.

You are **observing**.

Personal experiences

What do you think it's like to experience an earthquake or a volcanic eruption? Here are some examples of what people said about the events shown in the pictures.

EXPLORE

- Decide whether the statements in bubbles are **observations**, **inferences**, **hypotheses**, **interpretations** or **predictions**.
- Which situation is each person talking about?
- Was it before or after the event?

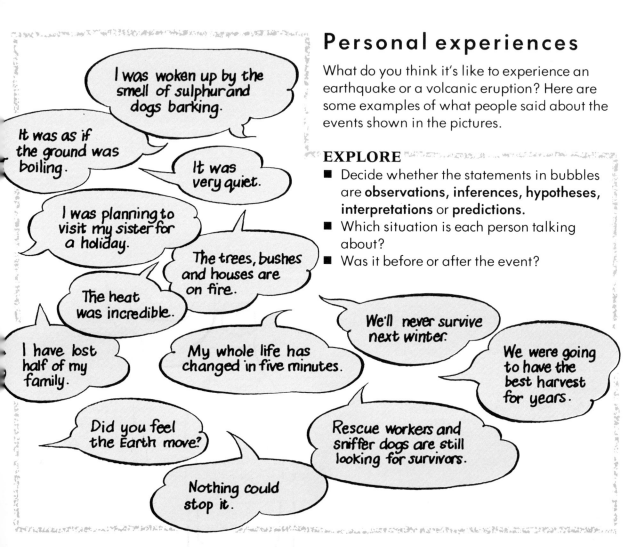

PRESENT

- Imagine you are experiencing an earthquake, a volcanic eruption or a tidal wave. You could be a journalist, a scientist, a nurse at the hospital, or an elderly person who finds it difficult to move. Use the information on this page to help you describe what happens. You could present your work as a newspaper article, a tape recording or a story.
These ideas may also help:

From our Science reporter
It was the strongest at 7.5 on the Richter
At least 50 thousand have died and many under collapsed build

What I saw and felt	What I did	What happened to friends, family and local people
There were strong vibrations I was surrounded by clouds of smoke. I felt scared.	I started running...	Some of my friends were killed, they got crushed in collapsed buildings.

ELEMENTS, MIXTURES AND COMPOUNDS

Have you ever read food labels carefully? Sometimes there's more to them than meets the eye.

EXPLORE

- Look at the labels and put the substances into groups. You are **classifying**.
- **Record** the names and contents of your groups. How did you make your classification?

Changing mixtures into compounds

Soap is a substance with an unusual property— it makes a foam when you rub it with water.
   This is how you make soap. ▼

1 You start with these substances.

2 You stir the substances to make a mixture.

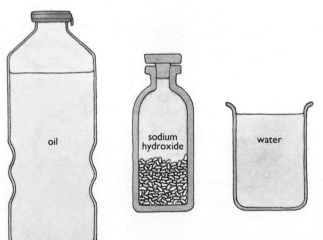

oil

sodium
hydroxide

water

EXPLORE

- What colours are the original substances?
- What colour do you think the mixture will be?

3 You heat the mixture to make a **compound** called soap.

4 You separate the soap from the mixture by adding salt to the curds and pouring off the liquid

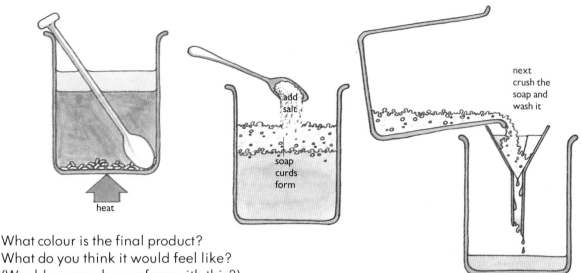

add salt

soap curds form

next crush the soap and wash it

heat

What colour is the final product?
What do you think it would feel like?
(Would you wash your face with this?)

EXPLORE
■ **Observe** each picture of making soap.
■ Copy and complete this chart for the substances in the pictures. You are **interpreting**.

What do you think advertisers mean when they say that soap is **pure**? Find out what an **element** is. Do you think soap is a compound, a mixture or an element?

	Mixture	Compound
Colour		
Texture		
Is heat energy used to make it?		
Could it be separated to the original substances?		

Mixtures always look a bit like the original substances they're made from – but compounds look really different.

Heat energy is put in or given out when they are made.

You can still separate these by physical means...

They can't be split into anything different from themselves.

The amount of each element you put in to make a compound must always be the same because...

These are always white...

EXPLORE
Here are some descriptions written by chemistry students about elements, compounds and mixtures.
■ Choose the best ones to write your own description of an element. Do the same for a mixture and a compound. Use reference books to help you.

PRESENT
■ Look back at the food labels. Now **classify** them as mixtures or compounds.
■ Redesign some of the labels so that people could tell whether each food was a mixture or a compound.

EXPERIMENTING WITH NUCLEAR POWER

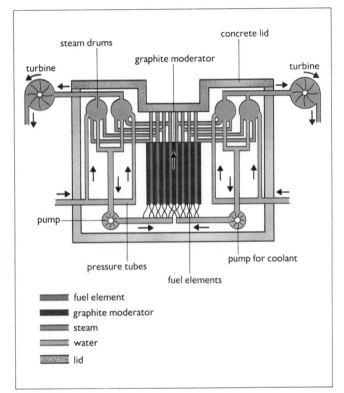

- steam drums
- concrete lid
- graphite moderator
- turbine
- turbine
- pump
- pressure tubes
- pump for coolant
- fuel elements

- fuel element
- graphite moderator
- steam
- water
- lid

Using radioactivity

What does the word **radioactivity** mean to you? Explosions, dangerous rays, lots of useful energy, medical diagnosis and treatment? Uranium is a radioactive element. Some atoms of it break up very quickly, setting free particles that can break up other atoms. It also releases energy when it breaks up. If the break-up is uncontrolled huge amounts of energy are released at one moment—this is **applied** in a *nuclear bomb*.

If we can control the break-up of uranium we can use the energy that is released to make electricity. The diagram shows a **nuclear reactor**. Graphite rods inside the reactor control the break-up of uranium. The graphite absorbs most of the particles and so stops the reaction getting out of control.

The amount of energy given out by this nuclear reactor can be controlled by moving the graphite rods up and down

A powerful experiment

At Chernobyl, in the USSR, an experiment with nuclear power went disastrously wrong. A nuclear scientist thought there would be enough energy in the generator turbine during shutdown to provide an emergency supply of electricity. Two other scientists decided to test this **hypothesis** with the following **experiment**. They put the reactor on to low power and removed the graphite rods. In a shutdown the safety systems would be off, so, to make it a fair test, they turned off the safety systems.

EXPLORE
- Do you think their experiment was well designed?
- **Predict** what happened.

The reactor at Chernobyl

You may already know what happened during this experiment at Chernobyl.
The reactor became hot. The graphite rods could not be replaced in the reactor. The nuclear reaction was no longer under control and an explosion occurred. The reactor lid was blown off and a fire began, which killed 30 people. A cloud of radioactive steam was released into the atmosphere.

EXPLORE

- Was this experiment worth doing?
- Is the scientific method always useful?

Why is radiation dangerous?

Radioactive substances give off radiation. Radiation harms the cells in the body. People who are exposed to a large amount of radiation die quickly of radiation sickness. Smaller amounts of radiation may cause cancers in affected cells. You cannot see radiation, though it can pass through solid objects. There are three main types of radiation. The diagram shows what they can pass through, and what stops them.

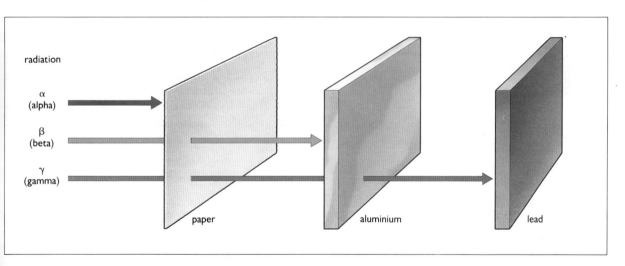

EXPLORE

To answer these questions you will need to **interpret** the diagram.

- Which type of radiation is most easily stopped?
- Which type of radiation is most difficult to stop?
- Which type of radiation can be stopped by some metals but not by others?
- Which type of radiation would only be dangerous to people if they swallowed it?

PRESENT

- Write a five-minute interview for Radio 1 between yourself and a nuclear scientist to explain how a nuclear reactor works. Make the interview both interesting *and* informative.

GASES

There are gases in the air all around you. You can feel them when the wind blows, and you breathe them all the time. But how do you get hold of them and investigate them?

A photo story

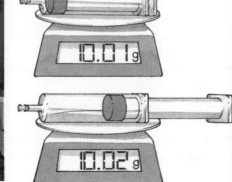

How would you know how much steam to put in? You wouldn't know how much it weighed until you had weighed it.

And the steam would cool down and condense when it got into the syringe. Then it wouldn't be steam any more but water.

Well, couldn't you build a jacket or something round the syringe to keep it warm, like in this diagram?

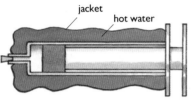

jacket   hot water

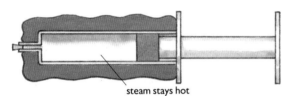

steam stays hot

Then it wouldn't be a fair test. You'd have to have the ice and the water hot when you weighed them.

And temperature makes a big difference to gases, look how bread rises when you heat it up – that's the gas bubbles getting bigger.

And another thing that would make the syringe idea difficult is how smooth they are. Some syringes move out smoothly with just a little bit of pressure. Some of them stick and you'd need to put a lot of pressure on them – so if you put steam in the syringe that needed a lot of pressure, you'd get a different amount to one with a little pressure.

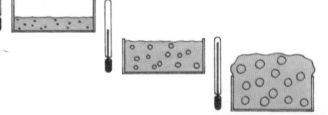

Okay, Okay. I wish I'd never asked.

Gosh, I am glad we tolerate uncertainty.

EXPLORE

- There are lots of different ideas here. Make a list of them.
- Write beside each idea whether you agree, disagree or don't know.
- Write your own account of how to weigh gases.

GASES IN THE AIR

Air is there

You know that air is all around you. But *how* do you know? What *evidence* do you have? Jane's group were thinking about this problem. They made a poster of their ideas.

When they returned after half-term their poster had been ruined—a leaky roof!

EXPLORE

- Make a plan for another poster called 'Air is there—observations and inferences'.
- Decide what **observations** you can make from each picture that tell you air is involved.
- What **inferences** about air can you make from each picture? These ideas might help you.

I know air is there because things keep...

The flag is flapping because...

Air makes things move...

The washing flaps because...

The hair is blowing because...

The waves have white tops...

When things move it means...

In the air

In their work on air Jane's group also found that air was a mixture of gases. They found this chart about gases in the air. ▼

Dry air is made up of these gases ▼

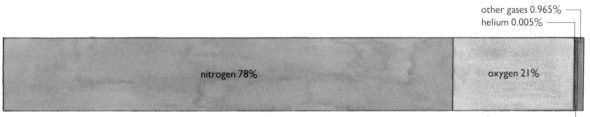

other gases 0.965%
helium 0.005%
nitrogen 78%
oxygen 21%
carbon dioxide 0.03%

They decided to add these figures to their poster. They thought a pie chart would make the figures easier to understand. They made lots of parts of the pie chart, but they got mixed up.

PRESENT

- Complete the pie chart for their poster. Cut Out TEB4 will help you.

The fun of the fair

At Easter the local fun fair was in the park near Jane's house. She bought two balloons filled with different gases. She knew that one was filled with oxygen and the other was filled with a mystery gas. One floated well, but the other one didn't.

EXPLORE

- Why might a balloon not float very well?
- If you had one balloon full of each of the gases in the chart, which balloons would not float well?
- What gas do you think is in the mystery balloon?

Gas	'Weight'
Oxygen	16
Carbon dioxide	22
Air	14.4
Helium	4
Hydrogen	1
Nitrogen	14

GETTING PURE METALS

Iron ore is extracted from the ground

Pure ore combined?

A few metals are found in the Earth as the pure metal, such as gold. Most combine with other chemicals to form compounds in the Earth called **ores**. Metals often combine with oxygen—the combining process is then called **oxidation**. The compounds formed with oxygen are **oxides**. **Iron** ore contains iron oxides. In order to use the metal we have to remove it from the ore.

Getting pure iron

Iron oxide is heated in a huge furnace with *carbon* (which is in the form of coke). At high temperatures carbon combines with oxygen to form *carbon dioxide*. The carbon is **oxidised** (carbon dioxide is an oxide containing two atoms of oxygen).

iron oxide + carbon → iron + carbon dioxide

To make the furnace hot enough, huge blasts of air are pumped through it. This is how it gets its name—the **blast furnace**.

Iron oxide is converted to iron in a blast furnace

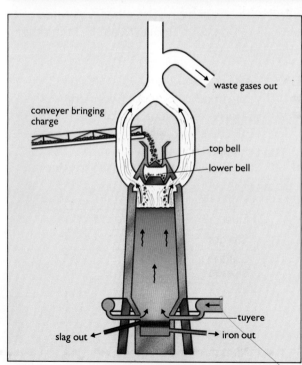

conveyer bringing charge

waste gases out

top bell

lower bell

tuyere

slag out

iron out

Getting pure aluminium

People have been making pure iron for many thousands of years. **Aluminium** is much more difficult to make, even though there is more of it in the Earth.

Aluminium is oxidised like iron, and it combines with oxygen very strongly. People tried heating aluminium oxide with coke, but this did not work.

To remove the oxygen from aluminium oxide you have to use electricity. This process is known as **electrolysis**. Elelctrolysis of aluminium oxide was not used until 1886. It has to be done at a high temperature, so that the aluminium oxide is a liquid—aluminium oxide does not conduct electricity when it is a solid.

Electrolysis breaks the aluminium oxide into aluminium and oxygen.

aluminium oxide → aluminium + oxygen

The process uses a lot of electricity—18 000 kilowatt-hours are needed to make one tonne of aluminium.

What happens in electrolysis

Why do you think this aluminium works is by a power station?

Molten aluminium is taken from the electrolysis can

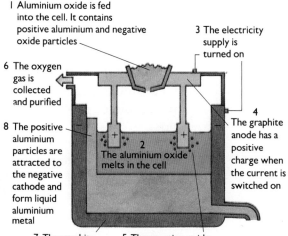

1 Aluminium oxide is fed into the cell. It contains positive aluminium and negative oxide particles

3 The electricity supply is turned on

6 The oxygen gas is collected and purified

4 The graphite anode has a positive charge when the current is switched on

2 The aluminium oxide melts in the cell

8 The positive aluminium particles are attracted to the negative cathode and form liquid aluminium metal

7 The graphite lining has a negative charge when the current is switched on

5 The negative oxide particles are attracted to the positive anode and form oxygen gas

9 The liquid aluminium can be sucked out of the cell

EXPLORE

■ Draw a flow diagram showing what happens during the electrolysis of aluminium.

PRESENT

■ Imagine you are an aluminium particle. Describe your adventure from a block of aluminium oxide to a strip of aluminium foil.

■ Prepare a radio programme that explains the differences between making iron and making aluminium.

GLASS AND CERAMICS

Glass is made by heating together three chemicals — silicon dioxide (sand), sodium oxide (from soda) and calcium oxide (from limestone). These three chemicals are widely available, so glass is a fairly cheap material.

Ceramics include anything made from clay. The clay is shaped when it is wet, then dried at a high temperature. Bricks and tiles can be made from raw clay, but clay for plates and cups has to be carefully purified before it is used.

EXPLORE

- Each object in this picture can be made from different materials. Think of two different materials for each object.

Why are windows made of glass?

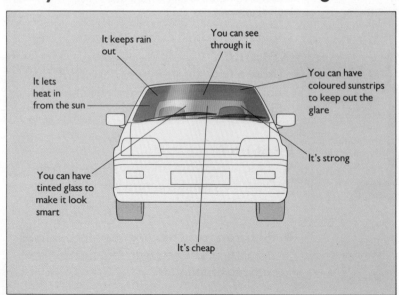

It keeps rain out

You can see through it

You can have coloured sunstrips to keep out the glare

It lets heat in from the sun

It's strong

You can have tinted glass to make it look smart

It's cheap

EXPLORE

- Draw a diagram like this for each of the objects in the picture above that you think could be made of glass.
- When you have finished the diagrams, try to put the reasons in order of importance for each one.

This star diagram shows some reasons for making a windscreen of glass

Making pottery

a Barry kneads the clay

b He spins it on a wheel

c He shapes it, then paints glaze onto it

d He puts it in a kiln (a very hot oven) to fire it. This makes the clay hard so the pot can be used

EXPLORE
- Look back at the star diagram on the last page. Make some similar diagrams for things that could be made of ceramics.

PRESENT
- Prepare a display for a local supermarket about making storage containers for food.
  Use Cut Out TEB6 to help you in the part about making bottles. Use the information in the photographs to show similar information about pots.

PERIODIC TABLE

Elementary, my dear . . .

How many elements can you think of? In fact there are 92 elements in the Earth. Trying to remember their names and what they all do is quite a headache. Over many years scientists have developed the Periodic Table, which helps.

EXPLORE

- List any similarities you can see in these elements. You are **observing**.
- List some differences you can see between the elements. You are **observing**.

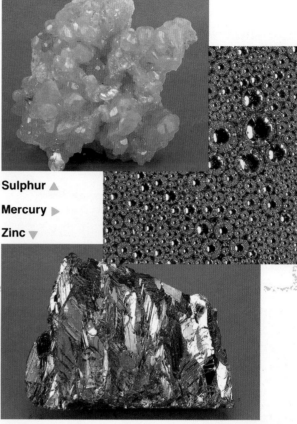

Sulphur ▲

Mercury ▶

Zinc ▼

Classified information

Some people use the Periodic Table to **classify** and arrange elements. The Periodic Table has vertical **groups** of elements and horizontal **periods** of elements.

These are some of the 92 elements found naturally in the Earth's surface

EXPLORE

- Find a copy of the Periodic Table. Which element in the pictures is in (a) Group VI, (b) Period 4, (c) Period 6? You are **interpreting** the Periodic Table.
- Find out about how the elements have been arranged in the Periodic Table. Use the element cards on Cut Out TEB7 to help.

1. Sort the elements into two groups: 'colourless' and 'coloured'. You are **classifying**.
   Find the positions of the elements on the Periodic Table. Do you notice a pattern? Describe it.

2. Rank the cards in order with the highest melting point at the top. Describe any pattern you can see.

3. **Classify** the cards into 'metals' and 'non-metals'. Describe any pattern you can see.

4. Classify or rank the cards in other ways to find other patterns. Use some of these ideas to start you off:

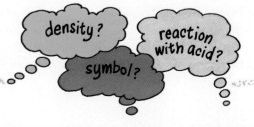

density?

symbol?

reaction with acid?

Periodic patterns?

Arun's group were discussing the patterns they had found in the Periodic Table. These were their **hypotheses**.

EXPLORE
- Which ones do you agree with?
- Add some of your own.
- Write a list of patterns in your book.

> Metals are found on the left hand side of the Periodic Table.

> Elements in the same period have the same density.

> Non-metals are solids at room temperature.

> Non-metals are less dense than metals.

> Metals float on water.

> Elements in Period II are non-metals.

> Metals are shiny and grey.

> Metals produce hydrogen gas when they react with acid.

Group II

Be	beryllium
Mg	magnesium
Ca	calcium
Sr	strontium
Ba	barium
Ra	radon

Beryllium

Magnesium

Group photos

Pick out the cards for the elements in Group II of the Periodic Table. They are in the same group because they have similar properties.

EXPLORE
- Use the cards and photos to make a list of the properties of Group II elements.
- List the differences between the Group II elements. You are **interpreting**.
- Write your own card for calcium (Ca) using the other Group II cards to help you. You are **applying** what you have learnt to make **predictions**.
- Use the photos and cards to list the properties of Group VII elements.
- Write a card for chlorine (Cl) using the other Group VII cards to help you.
- Use a chemistry book or encyclopaedia to check your **predictions**.

Group VII

F	fluorine
Cl	chlorine
Br	bromine
I	iodine

Bromine

Iodine

PRESENT

A lab technician found five bottles of elements in the cupboard. The names had been replaced with the letters A–E. The melting points were still on the labels. The lab technician did some tests.

- Make a large table telling the lab technician what you can **infer** about each element. Include whether you think it is a metal or non-metal, where it might be found in the Periodic Table and any other information that might be useful.

Element	Melting point (°C)	Does it conduct electricity?	Reaction with acid
A	1083 °C	yes	rapid
B	-219 °C	no	none
C	44 °C	no	none
D	181 °C	yes	slow
E	-39 °C	yes	none

RAIN

Rained off

One day Tim was day dreaming about football during a science lesson about the water cycle. He was thinking about playing football at lunchtime but as he looked through the window he noticed that it was raining hard. There were puddles all over the playground, the drains were blocking up and the trees were dripping. An hour later Tim noticed that it had stopped raining, all the puddles had gone and the drains were clear.

Where has all the water gone?

Tim had these ideas.

Into the sky.

To the bottom of the playground.

Into the bricks of the buildings.

EXPLORE

- Where else do you think the water might have gone? Would it all have gone into the drains, or would some go somewhere else? You are **hypothesising.**
- Make a record of your ideas so far.

Mist again

Later that night Tim was having a shower. He noticed there was mist on the window when he finished.

▶

EXPLORE

- Where do you think the mist came from?
- What was it made of? You are **inferring**.
- An hour later all the mist had gone. Where do you think it went?

On and on

Tim's next science lesson was about the water cycle *again*.

Tim started doodling as his teacher was talking, but he didn't get his doodle finished.

1. Our rainwater could once have been ice or snow in the Himalayas

2. The Sun melts the ice or snow and turns it into water

.... and then this water travels down the mountains and makes rivers and lakes

3. The Sun or warm Earth warms up the water and makes it <u>evaporate</u>, or change into a gas called <u>water vapour</u>

4. Up in the clouds the gas <u>condenses</u> and changes back into water, or else it freezes and makes snow or ice

5. the water or snow travels around in the clouds until it falls on our playground as rain or snow.

PRESENT

- Finish Tim's doodle using what his teacher told him. Cut Out TEB8 will help.

EXPLORE

- Go back to your ideas about where the rain went. How do you want to change them?
- How could you measure how much rain fell on your playground?

PRESENT

- Imagine you were a water particle travelling in the water cycle for a day. Write a diary of what happened to you. These headings might help you.

Where I started	What I got changed into	What happened to me next

SOIL

A rocky start

You know that soil lets plants grow. It has a strange smell and a distinctive feel when you put your hands in it. But where does it come from? Will we ever run out of it?

In fact, soil is being made all the time from the rock covering the Earth's surface. It takes thousands of years to make soil from bare rock. Soil is made of tiny particles of rock and **humus**. Humus is the decayed remains of dead animals and plants.

EXPLORE

- What other living things do you know of that live in the soil?
- Soil is vital to everything that lives on land. Why do you think this is?

Soil there is to it

The photos show how soil is made from bare rock.

PRESENT

- The manager of a local garden centre wants an attractive and educational poster to liven up the tea bar. Make a large coloured diagram for her showing how soil is made. Use Cut Out TEB9 (Part 1) to help you.
  Underline in red where weathering takes place. Underline in green where humus is added to the soil. Make a key.

1. Rainwater soaks into the rock. If the water freezes, the rock cracks. Rainwater contains a weak acid which dissolves the rock. The rock expands in the hot sun and contracts during cold nights, making the cracks bigger. The effects of temperature and rain are called **weathering** ▽

2. Small plants grow in the cracks. When they die they add humus to the cracks ▽

3. The weathering continues for thousands of years and breaks the rock into smaller and smaller pieces. Larger plants grow in the weathered rock and add to the humus when they die ▽

4. The small pieces of rocks mix with humus to make soil. Some rock pieces are washed into rivers and worn ◁ down into small particles of sand and clay

What sort of soil?

We can **classify** soil by the size of its particles.

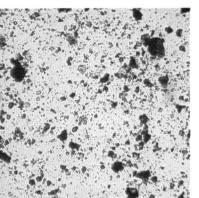

Clay soil ▲

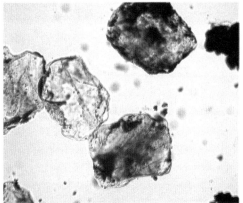

Sandy soil ▲

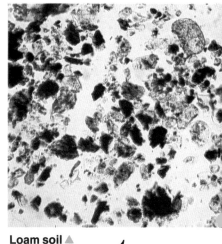

Loam soil ▲

Phil's group were discussing the photos.

The particles are very small.

The air spaces are large.

The particles are mixed sizes.

Water will drain through easily.

EXPLORE

■ Which statements are **observations** and which are **inferences**? Add some of your own.

Soil	Diagram	Observation	Inferences	Other points
Sandy				
Clay				
Loam				

PRESENT

■ Some people who come to the garden centre are confused about clay, sand and loam soils. Make a large table to summarise all the information about soil types. Use Cut Out TEB9 (Part 2) to help you.

Other differences

The type of soil also depends on the rock it's made from. The chemicals in the rock dissolve in the water and become part of the soil. Soils made from granite rock are usually slightly acidic. Soils formed from chalky rock are usually alkaline.

Most plants grow well in any soil if it is fertile and well dug. Some plants do best in certain conditions.

EXPLORE

■ What flowering plants do you know that seem to do well in most soils?
■ Which time of the year are they most colourful?

Plant	Position	Soil	Best time
holly bush	s or sh	any	all year
azalea	s or sh	a	summer
heather	s	a	all year
rhododendron	s or sh	a	all year, summer flowers
rose	s	any	summer flowers
iris	s	c	summer flowers
tulip	s	c	spring flowers
double daisy	s or sh	c	spring flowers
crabapple tree	s	n/c	autumn fruit
honeysuckle	s or sh	any	scented flowers

Key:
s=sun   a=acidic   c=chalk   sh=shade   n=neutral

TYPES OF ROCKS

Igneous rocks

Igneous rocks are usually formed when very hot molten material tries escaping from inside a volcano.

Basalt is an igneous rock

Granite is an igneous rock

EXPLORE
- Look at the photo of each type of igneous rock.
What can you say about how quickly each rock was cooled?

Solid as a rock?

You might think of rocks as big solid objects that nothing can change. In fact, they do change—but *very* slowly, over millions of years. You find rocks all over the place—on the beach, in the park, on a mountain, in the garden. Rocks from different places often look and feel different. You can **classify** them all into three types: igneous, sedimentary and metamorphic.

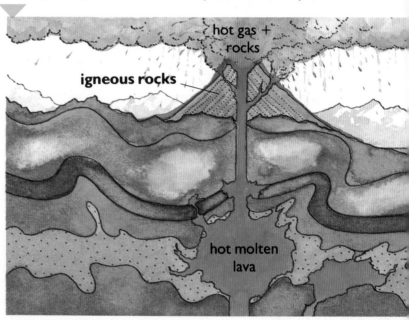

hot gas + rocks

igneous rocks

hot molten lava

Metamorphic rocks

Metamorphic rocks are usually made from other rocks. They are recycled rocks that have been changed by heat or pressure.

Marble is a metamorphic rock. Other examples are quartzite and slate

Sedimentary rocks

Sedimentary rocks have been formed over many thousands of years.

They have fine grains in them that have been squashed together over this long period of time.

EXPLORE
- Where might you find sedimentary rocks?
- **Predict** what they might feel like.

Sandstone is a sedimentary rock. Other examples are limestone and shale

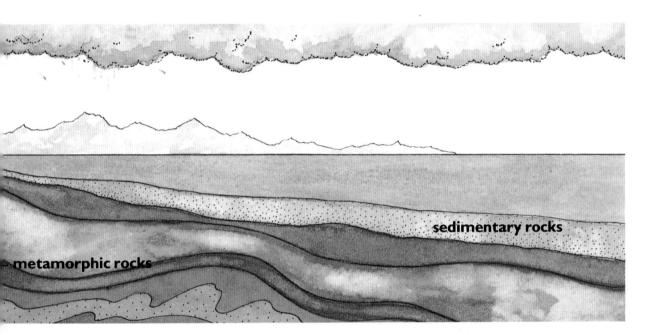

sedimentary rocks

metamorphic rocks

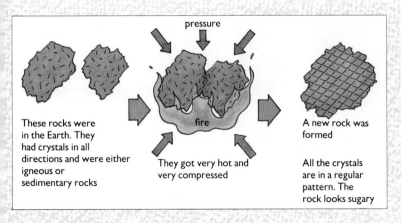

These rocks were in the Earth. They had crystals in all directions and were either igneous or sedimentary rocks

pressure

fire

They got very hot and very compressed

A new rock was formed

All the crystals are in a regular pattern. The rock looks sugary

How metamorphic rocks are made from other rocks

EXPLORE
- Which of the three types of rocks is made from recycling other rocks?
- Write about how each type of rock is formed. Use the information here and Cut Out TEB10 to help you.
- Look at any rocks that you or your school have. Use the information on these pages to help you **classify** them.

USING SYMBOLS

What are symbols used for?

You see symbols wherever you go, and you sometimes respond to them without even noticing them. People have been using symbols and signs for about two million years. Cave people drew symbols and the Ancient Egyptians had a complicated system of **hieroglyphics**—writing with pictures.

EXPLORE

- Where have you seen these symbols?
- What does each symbol mean?
- Why do you think we use symbols?
- Draw any other symbols you know and write down what they mean.
- Draw all the different symbols you have seen for a toilet.

Scientific symbols

The Periodic Table of elements is a system of scientific symbols. Part of the table is shown here. Each symbol represents an **element**.

H																	He
Li	Be											B	C	N	O	F	Ne
Na	Mg											Al	Si	P	S	Cl	Ar
K	Ca	Sc	Ti	V	Cr	Mn	Fe	Co	Ni	Cu	Zn	Ga	Ge	As	Se	Br	Kr

Coal is carbon. This model shows what one particle of carbon looks like. The symbol for carbon is C.

oxygen is a gas found in the air. This model shows what one particle of oxygen looks like. The symbol for oxygen is O.

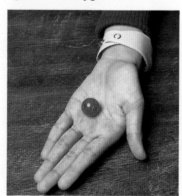

Usually two oxygen atoms join to make an oxygen **molecule**, O_2. A molecule is two or more atoms bonded together.

EXPLORE

- What do you think an element is?
- Make a list of the elements that you know with their symbols.

Compounding the theory

Not all the chemicals around us are elements. Elements combine to form **compounds**.

EXPLORE

- What do you think compounds are?
- Investigate other ways of representing elements and compounds. Cut Out TEB11 shows some of them.

Magnesium reacts with oxygen from the air . . .

Carbon reacts with oxygen in the air to form carbon dioxide, CO_2. The model shows what a particle looks like.

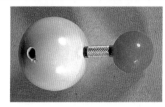

. . . to form magnesium oxide, MgO. The model shows what a particle looks like.

Which is which?

Tom's group were making some **observations** and **inferences** about elements and compounds. This is what they said.

EXPLORE

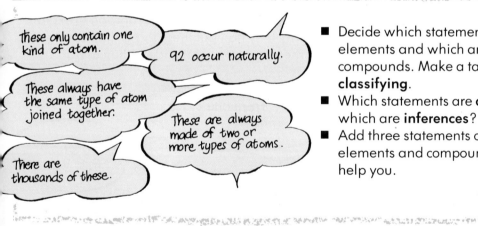

These only contain one kind of atom.

92 occur naturally.

These always have the same type of atom joined together.

These are always made of two or more types of atoms.

There are thousands of these.

- Decide which statements are about elements and which are about compounds. Make a table. You are **classifying**.
- Which statements are **observations** and which are **inferences**?
- Add three statements of your own about elements and compounds. Use a book to help you.

Word equations

You can represent what happens in chemical reactions by writing **word equations**. For example:

magnesium + oxygen → magnesium oxide

EXPLORE

- Play the equation game on Cut Out TEB12 to look at some more examples.

WHAT A STATE!

Water is a liquid. If you put water in the freezer, it turns to a solid—ice. If you boil water, it turns to steam. Solids, liquids, and gases are different **states**.

Which states are they?

Solids	Liquids	Gases
Wood	Water	
Ice		

EXPLORE

- Sam's group started to **classify** these objects into 'solids', 'liquids' and 'gases'. Complete a table like theirs.

They decided to write a paragraph to explain why they had put these things into each group. These are some of the ideas they used.

It stays in one place.

It flows from one place to another.

It's invisible.

It stays in a lump.

You can't feel it.

It's wet.

It's runny so it can change its shape.

It's heavy.

It's soft.

It's light.

It feels hard.

It can expand to fill up the space.

It can be squashed.

It's always the same volume.

EXPLORE

- Use the statements to write a paragraph that fully describes (a) solids, (b) liquids and (c) gases. Add some of your own statements.
- Look back to the 'solids, liquids and gases' table you drew. Write down any changes you want to make to your **classification**.

What's the difference?

Ayesha's group were discussing what makes solids, liquids and gases different. Which ideas do you agree with?

Ayesha found these diagrams in a book called *The easy guide to the kinetic theory*. It said that everything was made of very, very small particles.

Everything is made of particles. Ice and water are made of the same particles.

But water can turn into ice, and ice into water, so the particles can't be that different

That's silly - ice is made of ice particles and water is made of water particles.

EXPLORE

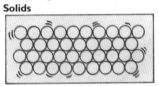

the particles are close together in a fixed pattern

Solids

the particles only move by vibrating because there are very strong forces between them

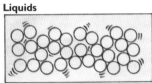

the particles are close together, but not in a fixed pattern

Liquids

the particles move easily although the forces between them are quite strong

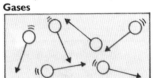

the particles are far apart with no fixed pattern

Gases

the particles move very fast because the forces between them are weak

- Which of your ideas fit in with this theory?
- Make a table to summarise the information about solids, liquids and gases. Use Cut Out TEB13 to help you.

Why are they different?

Look at each of these diagrams and read the reasons opposite.

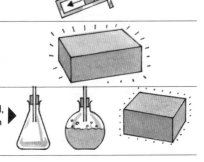

1
Most solids have a fixed shape, but liquids do not

2
A liquid can be poured, but a solid cannot

3
Solids and liquids cannot be squashed

4
Gases can be squashed easily

5
When a solid is heated it expands

6
When gases are heated, they expand more than solids and liquids

- because the particles in solids and liquids are packed close together
- because the particles in liquids can move more easily than the particles in solids
- because the particles in solids are closer together than in liquids

EXPLORE
- Match each reason with a picture. Write reasons for the three other pictures. **Record** your work.

PRESENT
- Persuade your teacher that *The easy guide to kinetic theory* does not tell the whole story.
Collect pictures or make drawings of things that do *not* fit easily into a solid, liquid or gas group. Present them on a poster and explain why they do not fit into the groups.

WHAT'S THE MATTER?

What's happening?

You know that things can be solids, liquids or gases—these are different **states**. But how do they change from one state to another? Why do some solids like salt and sugar, disappear when you put them in water?
Look at these pictures.

EXPLORE

- What name would you give to each process? You are **classifying**.
- Which pictures do you think show the same processes? You are **inferring**.
- Think of another example for each process you have identified.
- **Record** your name for each process and the examples in a table.

Some useful ideas

Over the years people have noticed these things happen. They have given names to their **observations**.

EXPLORE

When water goes from a solid to a liquid it is called melting

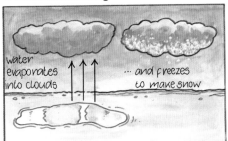

water evaporates into clouds

... and freezes to make snow

When water goes from a liquid to a solid it is called freezing

mist on bathroom window

When water goes from a gas to a liquid it is called condensation

When water goes from a liquid to a gas it is called evaporation

When a solid goes into water and makes a solution it is called dissolving

- **Record** the titles of the processes given here.
- Make rough sketches of the diagrams on the opposite page. Add one title you have recorded to each sketch.
- Label the changes happening in each sketch.
- Put the pictures into groups using the labels.
- Add some situations of your own to each group.
- How have your ideas changed from the activity on the opposite page?

A pinch of salt?

Brian and Adrian were having an argument about where the salt goes when it is put into potato water.

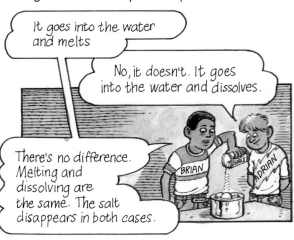

It goes into the water and melts

No, it doesn't. It goes into the water and dissolves.

There's no difference. Melting and dissolving are the same. The salt disappears in both cases.

BRIAN

ADRIAN

PRESENT
- How could you answer Brian? Draw some diagrams for him showing what happens to salt when it dissolves in water.

No, it doesn't. The salt's in the water all the time but you can't see it.

So what's the difference between melting and dissolving?

ADRIAN

BRIAN

WHEN DO THINGS EXPAND?

Have you ever noticed these things happening?

EXPLORE

■ Complete these sentences about what you think is happening in each picture.

The level in the thermometer goes up because . . .

People heat tin lids on jars if they're difficult to get off because . . .

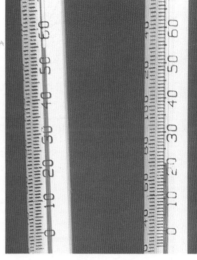

Bridging the gap

This is a story about what happened to a bridge.

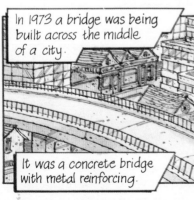

In 1973 a bridge was being built across the middle of a city.

It was a concrete bridge with metal reinforcing.

One night, after several weeks of very hot weather, the bridge collapsed.

They said it was because it had been so hot.

When they rebuilt the bridge they put metal teeth in it.

EXPLORE

■ Why do you think the bridge collapsed?
■ What did the builders have to do when they built the new bridge?
■ Why do you think bridges and overpasses are built with metal teeth?

Expanding the evidence

Here are some tests that Josie's group tried in the lab to help them understand what happens when things change size.

The ball went through the ring easily

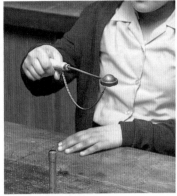

They heated the ball

The ball wouldn't go through the ring

As it cooled it went through the ring again

Here are some ideas they had to explain what happened.

The ball is a solid.

A solid that takes up more space has expanded.

Molecules move more quickly when they get hot.

Molecules that are moving quickly take up more space.

Some solids expand more quickly than others.

Perhaps we should try heating the hoop too, to make it fair.

Solids are made of molecules which move slowly.

EXPLORE
- Which of these ideas do you think help to explain what happened to the ball and ring?
- Add some ideas of your own.

PRESENT
- Write a conclusion for Josie explaining what happened to the ball and ring. Use the statements to help you.

The bimetallic strip—an expanding switch

A **bimetallic strip** is made of two strips of different metals joined together. When you heat the strip it bends. Bimetallic strips are used in electrical equipment like irons to control temperature.

EXPLORE
- Which of the two metals expanded more?
- Why do you think this happened?

PRESENT
- Produce a leaflet for a company making irons to explain to customers how the temperature of the iron is controlled. Use Cut Out TEB14 to help you. You are **applying**.

copper

iron

A copper/iron bimetallic strip

WHEN DO THINGS REACT?

Iron is used in sparklers

EXPLORE

- Apart from cost, why do you think we use certain metals for certain jobs?
- What do you think would happen if we used a different metal for the job shown here?

Some reactions of metals

These photos show some of the reactions of iron (symbol Fe).

Pure iron

Iron left in air

Iron burned in air

Iron with hydrochloric acid

Iron with iron sulphate

These photos show some of the reactions of magnesium (symbol Mg).

Pure magnesium

Magnesium left in air

Magnesium burned in air

Magnesium with hydrochloric acid

Magnesium with iron sulphate

These photos show some of the reactions of copper (symbol Cu).

Pure copper

Copper left in air

Copper burned in air

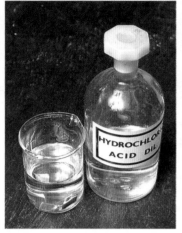
Copper with hydrochloric acid

Copper with iron sulphate

Comparing reactions

EXPLORE

- Make a chart for each metal showing how it reacts. Use the cards on Cut Out TEB 15 (Part 1) to help you. You are **interpreting**.
- Which metal do you think is the most reactive?
- Think about other metals you have studied. How did they react?

Metal.	Reaction in acid.	Reaction in air.	Reaction with iron sulphate.

- Copy this table. Put the metals in order, with the most reactive at the top. Include other metals you have studied as well.

More metals

Marlon's group were given this set of results.

Metal	Zinc (symbol Zn)
Reaction in acid	Reacts rapidly producing a steady stream of hydrogen bubbles
Reaction in air	Will only burn if it is ground to a fine powder
Reaction in iron sulphate	Zinc is more reactive so it pushes out the iron and makes zinc sulphate

EXPLORE

- Where would you put zinc in your reactivity table? You are **applying** what you have learnt.
- Lead is more reactive than copper, but less reactive than iron. Write a results card for lead. You are **applying** what you have learnt to make **predictions**.
- Check your **predictions** in a chemistry book. Make a new complete reactivity chart.

Rounding it up

Pam's group were discussing their reactivity chart.

> Metals always give off hydrogen when they react.

> Metals always form new chemicals when they react.

> The more reactive metals can push out the less reactive metals.

EXPLORE

- Which **hypotheses** do you agree with? Add some of your own and record them in your book.
- Look back at the first photo and questions on the opposite page. Have you changed any of your ideas?
- Write word equations to describe these chemical reactions. Cut Out TEB15 (Part 2) will help you.

WHERE'S IT GONE?

State to state

Energy makes things happen—if something changes then energy is probably involved. Do you think energy is involved when things change **state**—for example, going from a solid to a liquid, or from a gas to a liquid? These things are changing state.

EXPLORE

The washing is drying

Icebergs melt when it gets warmer

- What substance is changing state in each picture?
- Is the substance changing from a solid to a liquid, or a liquid to a solid, or something else? **Record** your ideas.

Energetic ideas

Here are some ideas about what happens when things change state.

Evaporation

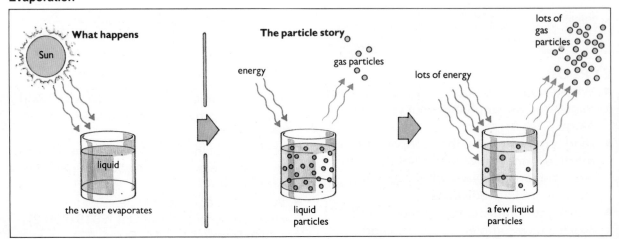

Diffusion

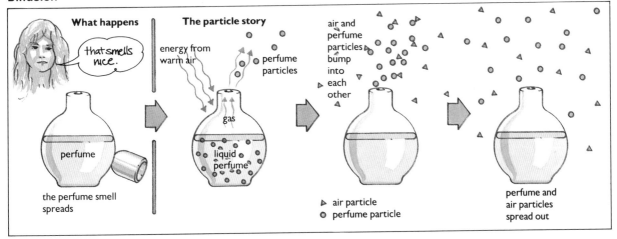

Melting

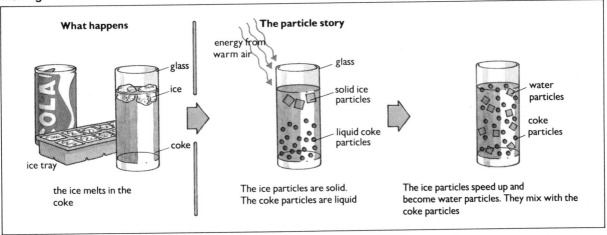

EXPLORE

- Match these descriptions to **evaporation**, **melting**, **diffusion**. You can use them more than once. Add some more descriptions of your own.

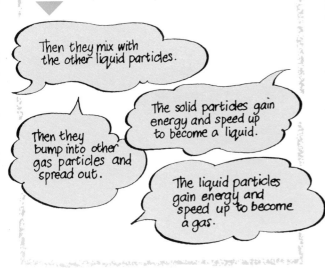

Then they mix with the other liquid particles.

Then they bump into other gas particles and spread out.

The solid particles gain energy and speed up to become a liquid.

The liquid particles gain energy and speed up to become a gas.

PRESENT

- Your school is having an open day. Make a poster for a display showing how things change state. Use the photos on the opposite page as examples. Cut Out TEB16 will help.

Not cabbage *again*

You can usually smell what's for school dinner a long time before you get to the canteen. Your friend says it makes him feel hungry!

PRESENT

- Make a diagram showing your friend how the smell has travelled from the kitchen to where you are in the school. Include your ideas about what changes state, what happens to the particles and where energy is involved.

WHY FARM HERE?

If you visit various parts of the UK you will notice that farmers use their land in different ways. Where might you go and see lots of sheep? Where would you be more likely to see wheat growing?
These pictures show two different farms.

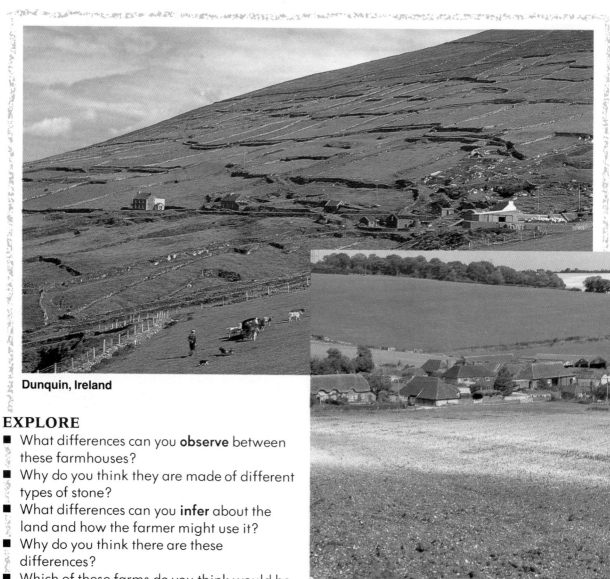

Dunquin, Ireland

Berkshire

EXPLORE

- What differences can you **observe** between these farmhouses?
- Why do you think they are made of different types of stone?
- What differences can you **infer** about the land and how the farmer might use it?
- Why do you think there are these differences?
- Which of these farms do you think would be worst affected by:
  (a) a drought,
  (b) a long winter with heavy snowfalls,
  (c) very high winds?

The root of the problem

Soils vary from place to place—their structures depend on the rocks they are made from. (There is more about this in Unit 2.15.) Different plants do well in different types of soil.

EXPLORE

Carrots grow well in sandy soil

Corn grows well in clay soil

- How do you think the two types of soil are different?
- How do you think these differences affect plants growing in them?

Rain—are you getting enough?

If these is too little water, plants will not grow and they may wither and die. With too much water, fields become waterlogged and unworkable.

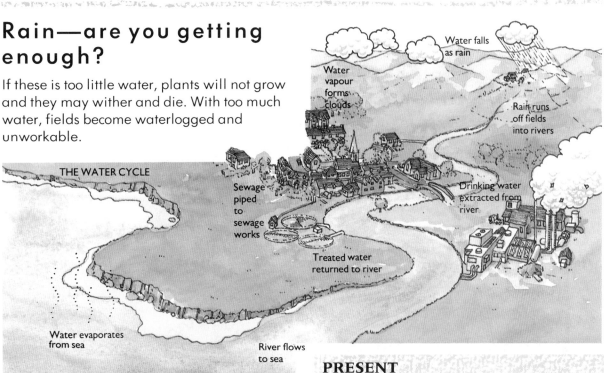

THE WATER CYCLE

Water falls as rain

Water vapour forms clouds

Rain runs off fields into rivers

Drinking water extracted from river

Sewage piped to sewage works

Treated water returned to river

Water evaporates from sea

River flows to sea

PRESENT

- A local agricultural college is making a video to promote its courses. Collect pictures of farms throughout the UK. Use them to present a short sample lecture about farming in the UK, how it varies from place to place and why. You could video record your lecture if you have a video camera available.

ACTION ADVENTURE
EVERYDAY MACHINES

EXPLORE

- How many different **machines** can you think of? Make a list.
- Why do you think we use machines? How do they help us?

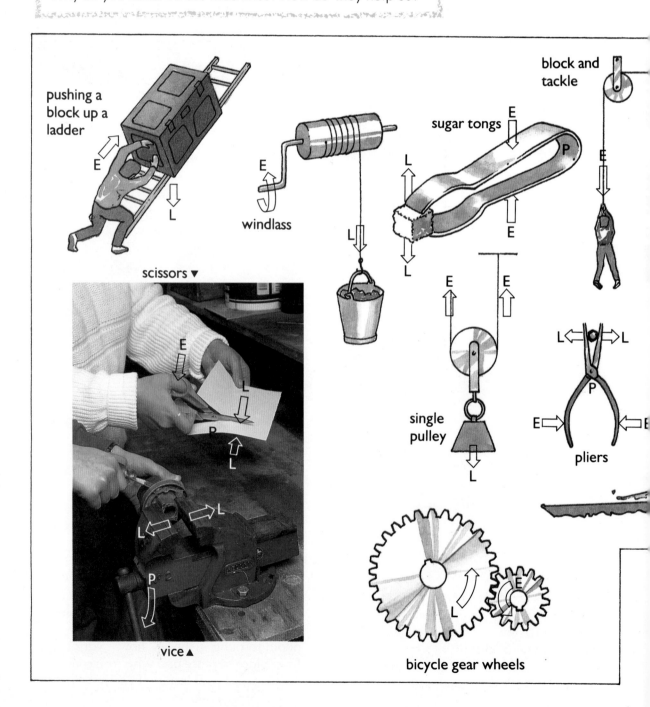

pushing a block up a ladder

windlass

scissors ▼

sugar tongs

block and tackle

single pulley

pliers

vice ▲

bicycle gear wheels

3.1

Making light work

If you move a force, for example lift a weight, you do **work**. Machines make it easier to do work by changing the effect of the forces involved. Some machines magnify the force you put in, so you don't have to push or pull so hard to get the same result. Others change the direction of the force you put in so, for example, instead of struggling to push upwards you can push downwards instead which is easier. The force you put in is called the **effort** (E). The force you are trying to move, for example the weight you are trying to lift, is called the **load** (L). In some machines there is a point which stays still while the forces move around it. This is called the **pivot** (P). In these machines the effort, load and pivot have been marked. ▼

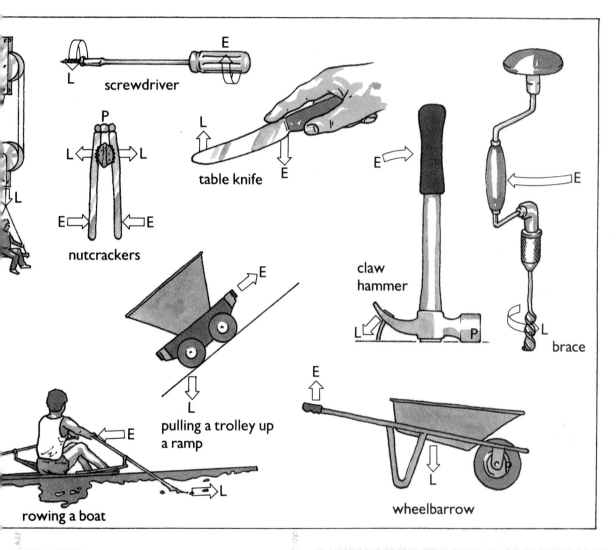

screwdriver

nutcrackers

table knife

pulling a trolley up a ramp

rowing a boat

claw hammer

brace

wheelbarrow

EXPLORE
- **Classify** these machines using the following headings: 'Levers', 'Ramps', 'Wheels and axles'.
- What other ways of **classifying** these machines can you think of? Show how each machine fits into your classification.

PRESENT
- Write a short story called 'Moving home'. In your story, describe what people use each of these machines for, and how they work. Show how the machines help people to do work (or how they are supposed to—do you think machines always work?).

FLOATING AND SINKING

Floating debris

Barry, Josette and Shona were helping an environmental group clean up the canal. They managed to find some time for scientific activity though! They were throwing things in the canal.

'It's easy to tell which things will sink', said Barry. 'You've only got to feel how heavy they are. The heavy ones sink and the light ones float.'

'Rubbish', said Shona. 'It's the size that's important. Look at all that small stuff floating over there—the big things sink straight away.'

'It must be to do with both size and heaviness', said Josette. 'It's not fair to compare a huge heavy thing with a small light thing.'

EXPLORE
- What was Barry's **hypothesis**?
- What was Shona's **hypothesis**?
- What was Josette's **hypothesis**?
- Which one do you agree with?

Sinking scientifically

Later on they had a chance to explore their ideas in the laboratory. They collected some objects and measured how big and how heavy each object was. Then they put them into a bowl of water.

They found the volume by lowering the objects into a measuring cylinder of water and recording the difference in the readings

They weighed the objects on a balance

They tested the objects in water

Here are their results:

<u>Mass</u>

Polished aluminium	81 g
Marble block	96 g
Escrim board	2 g
Aged oak	18 g
Etched copper strip	130 g
Xanthia wood	3 g
Lump of Iron	160 g

<u>Volume</u>

Xanthia wood	6 cm³
Lump of iron	20 cm³
Marble block	40 cm³
Etched copper strip	14 cm³
Polished aluminium	30 cm³
Aged oak	20 cm³
Escrim board	10 cm³

<u>Floating</u>

Escrim board and Xanthia wood floated easily. Aged oak just floated. All the others sank.

EXPLORE

■ Make a table of their results, with the following headings:

Name	Did it float	Mass (g)	Volume (cm³)	Density (g/cm³)

(To find the density you will need to divide the mass by the volume.

$$\text{Density} = \frac{\text{mass}}{\text{volume}}$$

You may find it helpful to use a calculator.)

■ Rank the materials in order of mass, starting with the lightest.
■ Rank the materials in order of volume, starting with the smallest.
■ Rank the materials in order of density, starting with the smallest density.
■ Which hypothesis do the results support?

Heavy metal?

'Lots of boats are made of iron', **observed** Barry. 'Our lump of iron sank, why do iron boats float?'
Shona and Chung thought that the shape of a boat was important, as well as what it is made from. As long as the volume of the boat (in cm³) is bigger than the mass of the boat (in g) it will float.

This tanker is made of steel

PRESENT

■ A multimillionaire has asked you to design a speedboat to cross the Atlantic in record time. Wood would break up at high speed, so choose one of the metals tested on this page. Make a drawing of your design showing the shape of the boat, its volume, what it's made of and its mass. Make sure your boat will float!

GETTING HOTTER

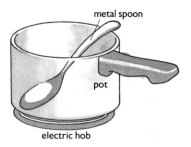

metal spoon

pot

electric hob

If you have ever been up in the loft on a hot day you will know that heat rises. But if you lie on a beach on a sunny day you get hot too. Leaving a poker in the fire and accidentally touching the other end will tell you that heat travels along pokers! How do you think the heat moves in each case?

Heating along lines and in circles

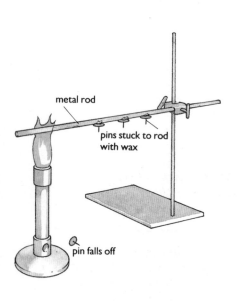

metal rod

pins stuck to rod with wax

pin falls off

smoke

fire

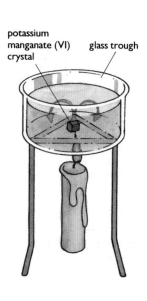

potassium manganate (VI) crystal

glass trough

Heat is travelling through solids, liquids and gases in these pictures

EXPLORE

■ For each diagram, decide whether the object that is getting hot is a solid, a liquid or a gas. Steve's group were looking at these diagrams and trying to describe what happens in **conduction** and **convection**. Here are some of the ideas they had.

■ Sort them into ideas that you agree with, disagree with or are not sure about.

■ Write some of your own.

■ Choose the best ones and join them together to complete these sentences:
  ● Conduction is . . .
  ● Convection is . . .

In convection, heat energy is absorbed.

In conduction, heat energy moves along a solid.

In convection, heat energy moves around in circles.

In conduction the molecules in a solid bump toge and move the hea along.

In convection, cold water won't move because it's not heated.

In conduction, heat energy rises.

In convection, heat energy moves by hot air or liquid rising and being replaced by cool air or liquid.

Heating through nothing

Heat from the Sun has to travel through space to get to us, so it can't move by conduction or convection. It is transferred by **radiation**. Any object which is hotter than its surroundings radiates heat.

EXPLORE

- What happens when things radiate heat energy? These are your **observations**.
- Which of these ideas do you think are correct **inferences** for the pictures above?
- Use your ideas to complete this sentence:
  - Radiation is . . .

> The person in shorts is radiating heat energy from the Sun.

> The person in shorts is moving the radiant heat energy about.

> The person in the woolly hat is radiating heat energy.

> The wall is radiating heat energy.

> The grass is radiating heat energy.

Ever been hot?

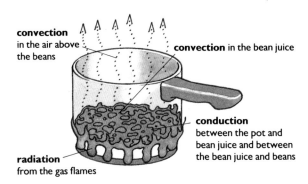

convection in the air above the beans

convection in the bean juice

conduction between the pot and bean juice and between the bean juice and beans

radiation from the gas flames

PRESENT

- The electricity board are producing a leaflet explaining how energy can be saved, and they want to start off by showing how heat travels. Make diagrams like this one for the first page of the leaflet to explain how things heat up and cool down. Cut Out AA1 will help you.

▶ **Conduction, convection and radiation can all work together to heat things up or cool them down**

GLOBAL ENERGY SOURCES

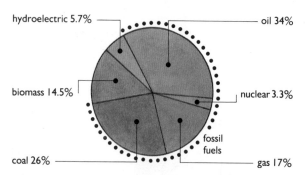

hydroelectric 5.7%

oil 34%

biomass 14.5%

nuclear 3.3%

coal 26%

fossil fuels

gas 17%

This pie chart shows energy sources that are used throughout the world

Running low

Some of the energy sources we use will eventually run out—they are **non-renewable**. We can **predict** when they will run out from how much we are using, and how much we know is still in the Earth. We might find new sources, for example new coal fields, but we are using much more than we are finding.

Other sources are **renewable**—they will not run out.

EXPLORE
- Which of the sources on the pie chart are renewable?
- Does the world use more renewable or non-renewable energy sources?
- Which sources will run out first?
- Make a table of energy sources using these headings.
- What could you do yourself to stop non-renewable energy sources running out?
- What could the country do to stop non-renewable energy sources running out?
- Who do you think is responsible for deciding which energy sources we should use?

EXPLORE
- How many ways can you think of that you use energy at home?
- How does the energy you use get to your home?

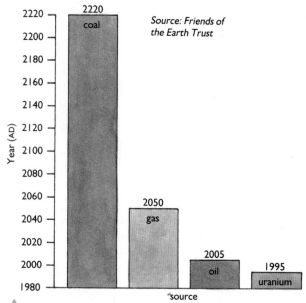

Source: Friends of the Earth Trust

2220 coal
2050 gas
2005 oil
1995 uranium

Year (AD)
source

This chart shows predictions of when non-renewable energy sources will run out

Source	Amount used in the world (%)	Renewable or non-renewable	When it might run out

PRESENT
- An environmental group have asked you to give a talk at a local meeting about conserving non-renewable energy sources. Prepare a speech explaining the problem and telling people what they can do, and what they could ask their MP to do.

A measure of energy

We often measure energy in joules (J). Because a joule is a small unit, we use petajoules (PJ) when talking about energy sources.

1 petajoule = 1 million billion joules = 10^{12}J

In a match there are about 4 J of energy ▲

◀ 376 000 tonnes of coal give 1 PJ of energy

What do we do with it all?

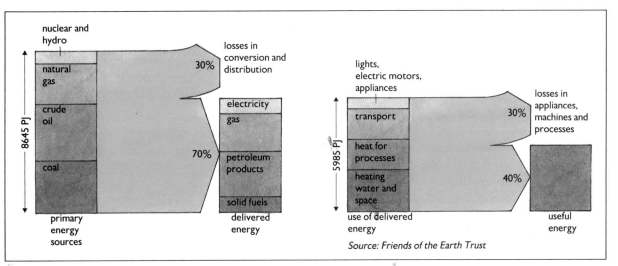

This diagram shows what happened to the energy used in the UK in 1985

EXPLORE

- What do you think 'primary energy sources' and 'delivered energy' mean?
- What percentage of energy was lost in changing from primary energy sources to delivered energy?
- How many petajoules is that?
- How much useful energy did we get from 8645 PJ of primary energy?
- What percentage of energy has been lost?
- How do we use most of the delivered energy?

PRESENT

- How do you think we can use energy more efficiently? Write a letter to the managing director of a local company suggesting how the company could waste less energy.

GRAVITY

Why do things fall *down*?

You will have **observed** that things fall towards the Earth. That's how you know where 'down' is—it's the direction things fall in. 'Up' is the opposite direction.

But why do things fall down, and not up or sideways? Until 1666 most people accepted that the universe was made that way, and did not question why down was down and not up! Then Isaac Newton made an **inference**: 'things fall towards the Earth because the Earth is pulling them towards it'.

The theory of gravity

Isaac Newton went on to work out a theory that explained not only why apples fell to the ground, but also why the Moon was in orbit around the Earth and why the Earth was in orbit around the Sun. It involved the force called **gravity**, that large masses, including the Earth, exert on other things.

The theory says:

'All things are attracted to one another by the force of gravity. How big the force is depends on how close together the things are and how massive they are. The force is greatest when things are near and have a large mass.'

EXPLORE

■ Make a series of diagrams showing what factors affect the force of gravity between two objects. Cut Out AA2 will help you.

The force of gravity between two objects depends on the mass of the objects and the distance between them

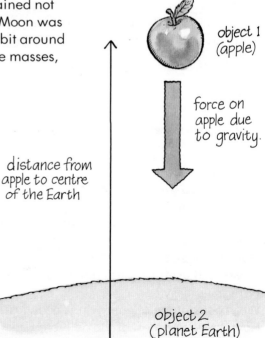

object 1 (apple)

force on apple due to gravity.

distance from apple to centre of the Earth

object 2 (planet Earth)

Masses of weight?

What's the difference between **mass** and **weight**? If you took an object with a mass of 100g to another planet, its mass would not change. An object's mass depends on the amount of stuff in it.

However, the object's weight would change on another planet. Weight is a force, and it depends on the mass of the object and the pull of gravity on it. On the Moon, the pull of gravity is one-sixth of the Earth's, so there the same object has one-sixth its Earth weight. And in space, where there is hardly any gravity pull at all, it will be 'weightless'.

These ideas were worked out by Isaac Newton, so weight and other forces are measured in units called **newtons**.

A mass of 100g would weigh slightly more on Saturn than on Earth—Saturn's gravity is a bit stronger than Earth's

Why do paper darts fly?

Milton had been reading about gravity. 'When I throw a paper dart, why doesn't the force of gravity pull it down straight-away?' he asked. 'Why does it wait for 20 or 30 seconds, and then pull it down?'

Isaac Newton's explanation would have been as follows:

1. Any object keeps moving at a steady speed a force acts on it.
2. When Milton throws the dart it moves at a steady speed, but the air gradually slows it down.

3. While the dart is moving, air flowing over the wings produces a force that lifts the dart. The lifting force cancels out the pull of gravity.
4. When the air has slowed the dart down there is no longer any lifting force.
5. Without lift to oppose it, the force of gravity now pulls the dart towards the centre of the Earth.

PRESENT
- Klog's want to put a plan for a paper dart on a cereal packet. Design a paper dart that will fly well. Convince them they should choose your design by explaining how the dart flies, and showing the forces involved.

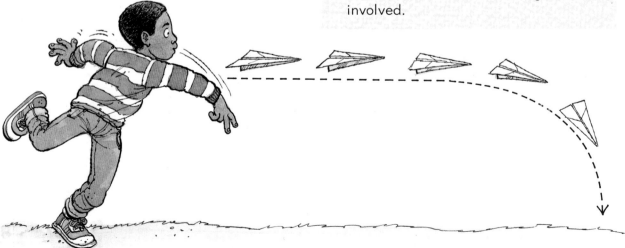

INSULATION

Save it

People talk a lot about saving or conserving energy at home. Why is this a good idea? How do you think we can do it?

Losing heat

This photograph is taken from the air by a special process. It shows a house and the amount of heat energy radiating from it.

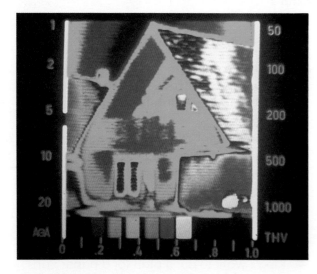

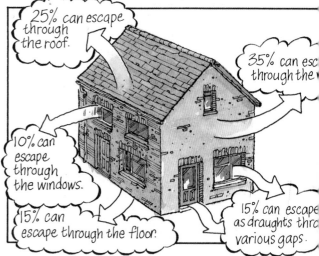

25% can escape through the roof.

35% can esc through the

10% can escape through the windows.

15% can escape through the floor.

15% can escape as draughts thro various gaps.

This diagram shows how heat escapes from a house

EXPLORE
- Which colour shows greatest heat?
- Which colour shows least heat loss?

You are **interpreting**.

- Which part of the house loses the most heat energy?
- Which part of the house loses the least heat energy?

You are **interpreting**.

- In which part of the house do you think it would be easiest to stop the heat energy loss? You are **predicting**.

EXPLORE
- Which colour shows greatest heat?
- Which colour shows least heat loss?

You are **interpreting**.

Keeping it in

The pictures here and on the next page show how people reduce heat energy losses through different parts of their houses.

They put insulation in the loft

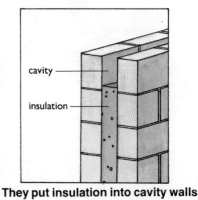

cavity

insulation

They put insulation into cavity walls

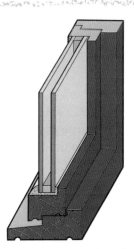

They put double-glazed windows in

EXPLORE

- For each of the four pictures decide whether the method reduces heat loss by conduction, convection, radiation, or a mixture of these. You are **applying** your ideas.

They draught-proof doors and windows

The cost of conservation

The table shows the reduction in heat loss for each method of insulation. The **pay-back time** is the time it takes to save the money you spent putting in the insulation, because of lower heating bills.

Method of insulation	Heat saved through that part of the house	Pay-back time
Roof insulation	80%	1 year
Cavity wall insulation	60–70%	3 years
Double glazing	50%	30–40 years
Draught-proofing	50–60%	6 months

Amount of heat lost through roof = 25%
Reduction through insulation = 80%
∴ Heat saved when roof is insulated = $\frac{80}{100} \times 25\%$
= 20%
∴ amount of heat lost through insulated roof = 25 - 20% = 5%

EXPLORE

- Imagine you are a student on a very low budget in a rented room. Which type of insulation would you put in to quickly save you money?
- If you were buying a house and had saved some money, which type of insulation might you put in first, second and third?
- What other things might architects think of to design houses which conserve energy, apart from insulation?

PRESENT

- Make a poster to persuade people to insulate their houses.
- Do calculations like the one here to work out how much heat energy is lost through other parts of the house after insulating them.
- Draw a picture of a house like the one on the opposite page. Mark on it the amount of heat lost if the four types of insulation have been used.

MAKING ELECTRICITY

When you flick an electric light switch, the bulb comes on. You know that the electricity comes from a power station—but how is it made? These pictures show how Michael Faraday discovered how to make electricity.

EXPLORE

■ Write a poem or rap called 'I'm all charged up' by Michael Faraday.

Hi! I'm Michael Faraday and I'm interested in the *observations* made by Hans Oersted and André Ampère.

HANS OERSTED IS [IN] [OUT]

The electric current affects the compass needle-just like a magnet.

ANDRÉ AMPÈRE IS [IN] [OUT]

These parallel wires repel when the current is on- just like a magnet

REPEL!
REPEL!

My *question* is this- if electricity in wires can produce a magnet, can we reverse the process and make a magnet produce electricity?

So, to try out this idea, I shall make a magnet in this wire...

...and see if it makes a magnet in this wire.

No chance! You need a more powerful magnet.

Right! Let's coil up the wire to make the magnet more powerful. Let's coil **both** wires to increase the effect.

And so - as we stand on the threshold of this historic experiment, Michael Faraday closes the switch that sends a current through the first wire. The ammeter in the second circuit twitches... and stops. The experiment has failed!

Hmmm! Well, there was a circuit there when we switched it on, and when we switched it off.

But not the rest of the time. Admit it Mike— it **didn't work!**

Well, perhaps! Or perhaps it's the *movement* of the magnetic field when the current switches on and off that makes the second current.

A fortunate failure?

Faraday went on to show that this last **interpretation** was correct. Even though his experiment had not gone as **predicted**, his **observations** led to a completely new theory—the theory of **electromagnetic induction** (or 'how to make an electric current using magnets').

EXPLORE

- Make a series of diagrams and sentences in your book explaining how electromagnetic induction happens. Cut Out AA3 has some diagrams and sentences to help you. They describe another of Michael Faraday's induction experiments.

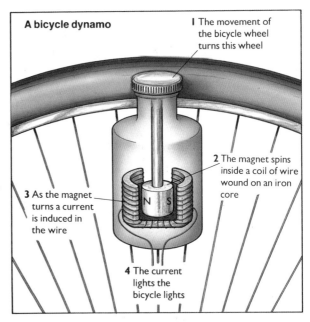

A bicycle dynamo

1 The movement of the bicycle wheel turns this wheel

2 The magnet spins inside a coil of wire wound on an iron core

3 As the magnet turns a current is induced in the wire

N S

4 The current lights the bicycle lights

Producing an electric current

The idea of using moving magnets to make electricity is **applied** in the dynamo.

EXPLORE

Using a lamp with a dynamo is not the only way to put lights on a bicycle.

- What other ways are there?
- What are the advantages of a dynamo compared with other systems?
- What are the disadvantages of a dynamo?

PRESENT

- Use the ideas you have explored to design a magazine advertisement for dynamos.

In a power station, current is induced by turbines. These have large magnets which turn inside the coils.

PHOTOSYNTHESIS

Lisa's group were doing some work on plants and energy. They found out that plants need certain things to grow. This is their diagram.

the plant uses Carbon dioxide from the air to make food

light from the sun gives plants energy, they use energy as they make food

food which is made in the leaves is carried around the plant to make it grow

the plant uses water to make food

chemicals in the soil help the plant to grow

Their teacher then talked to them about their experiments.

'What have you concluded from your results so far, Lisa?' she asked.

'Well, we think that plants need sunlight . . .'

'. . and water', piped up Sharon.

'Yes, and water to grow. But we don't know how they use the sunlight and water to make food', said Lisa.

'Well, I'll help you. Plants make sugars which are quickly changed into starch', said the teacher.

'So we could test the plants for starch', said Lisa.

'Yes, and you could do some more tests to find out if there are other things that plants need to make starch. But don't forget to make it a fair test', suggested the teacher.

Here are some tests they did.

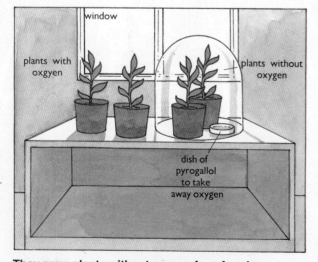

window

plants with oxgyen

plants without oxygen

dish of pyrogallol to take away oxygen

They grew plants without oxygen for a few days

They grew plants without carbon dioxide for a few days

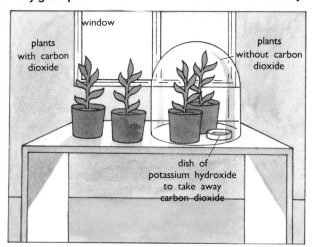

window

plants with carbon dioxide

plants without carbon dioxide

dish of potassium hydroxide to take away carbon dioxide

We left all the plants in the light. We also tried watering some plants but they just died. Our other results were:

Condition	Results after 5 days Starch present or not
with oxygen	✓
without oxygen	✓
with carbon dioxide	✓
without carbon dioxide	✗
with soil	✓
without soil	✓
in a hot room	✓
in a cold room	✓

EXPLORE

■ Look at the results of Lisa's group's experiments and decide what they found out. Use Cut Out AA4 to help you. You are **interpreting**.

PRESENT

■ Lisa's teacher told them that plants make food by a process called **photosynthesis**. Her group decided to make a collage of what happens in photosynthesis. This is how they started. Make a collage like it and finish it for them.

Then they tested their plants for starch ▼

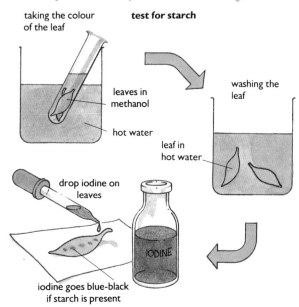

taking the colour of the leaf

test for starch

leaves in methanol

hot water

washing the leaf

leaf in hot water

drop iodine on leaves

IODINE

iodine goes blue-black if starch is present

Our teacher also showed us how to test the gas made by a water plant. We got these results:

Gas	Present or not
oxygen	✓
carbon dioxide	✗
hydrogen	✗

oxygen

light energy

water

carbon dioxide

3.8

SCENES FROM THE HISTORY OF MAGNETISM

We use magnets in compasses to find our way, and they are also used in some electrical devices. Can you think of other uses for magnets? These pictures show how ideas about magnets have changed. (They are not in the correct order.)

PRESENT
- Make a poster about magnets for an exhibition in a science museum. Sketch these pictures in the order you think is correct, and include any other information you can find.

People were convinced by Gilbert's model. But further investigation raised new questions.

Walter Elsasser suggested a new *hypothesis*.

People who investigated lodestones found that an iron needle could be magnetised by stroking it with a lodestone.

If the needle was free to move it would turn until it was pointing north and south. This idea was applied by sailors so that they could tell which direction they were sailing in, even when they could not see land.

People wondered why the needle pointed north. The first *hypothesis* was that there was a mountain made of lodestone far away to the north...

...but as time went by and no such mountain was discovered people began to wonder if the idea was true.

SCIENCE AND SCIENTISTS

We often hear that a scientist has made a breakthrough in research, or invented a new product. What do you think a scientist is?

EXPLORE

■ Pick out the scientists in the following pictures. Make a list.

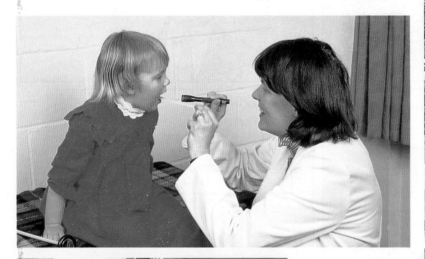

EXPLORE

- Share your decisions with your group. Did everyone agree?
- Which picture did most people choose?
- Which picture did least people choose?
- In fact, all seven pictures show scientists. Surprised? Show how they are all scientists. Cut Out AA5 will help you.

PRESENT

- Make a poster for a school open evening showing how science affects everyone.

SCIENCE IN ACTION

Julia and Lydia were tired of their parents bickering about the washing up

They identified a need to know which was the best value washing-up liquid

They sat down and planned what they would do . . .

They designed a test to see if there was a difference between the liquids . . .

They thought about the variables they would have to control

They persuaded a local supermarket to let them have some samples of washing-up liquids

This is what they got . . .

They carried out their plan, but with some changes . . .

Here are their results . . .

They gave their report to their parents and they all lived happily ever after

EXPLORE

- What other ways could you test washing-up liquids?
- Are there any other variables Julia and Lydia should take into account?
- Write a detailed plan of their experimental procedure.
- Present the data they obtained in tables.
- Use the data to produce a report on the washing-up liquids tested.

TRANSFERRING ENERGY

Bursting with energy

You need energy to move, breathe and grow. You also use energy at home and at school for heating, cooking and lighting. In fact, everything on the Earth that is alive, and anything else that moves, uses energy. Where does all this energy come from?

EXPLORE
- Make a chart using these headings about where energy comes from. You are **interpreting**.

% of sun's energy	Where it goes to	Is it useful?

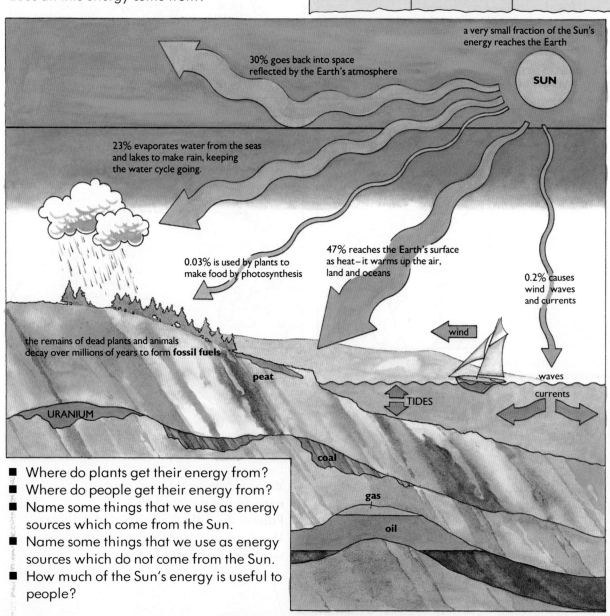

a very small fraction of the Sun's energy reaches the Earth

SUN

30% goes back into space reflected by the Earth's atmosphere

23% evaporates water from the seas and lakes to make rain, keeping the water cycle going.

0.03% is used by plants to make food by photosynthesis

47% reaches the Earth's surface as heat – it warms up the air, land and oceans

0.2% causes wind waves and currents

wind

waves

currents

the remains of dead plants and animals decay over millions of years to form **fossil fuels**

peat

TIDES

URANIUM

coal

gas

oil

- Where do plants get their energy from?
- Where do people get their energy from?
- Name some things that we use as energy sources which come from the Sun.
- Name some things that we use as energy sources which do not come from the Sun.
- How much of the Sun's energy is useful to people?

About 99% of energy on Earth comes from the Sun. The rest comes from inside the Earth and from the effect of the Moon and Sun on the oceans

Chains of energy

The Sun's energy makes other things which can then provide energy themselves. These energy sources give us *useful* energy.

EXPLORE
- Make some more energy chains. Use Cut Out AA6 to help you.

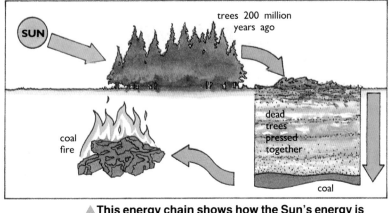

▲ **This energy chain shows how the Sun's energy is converted into coal we can burn to give us heat**

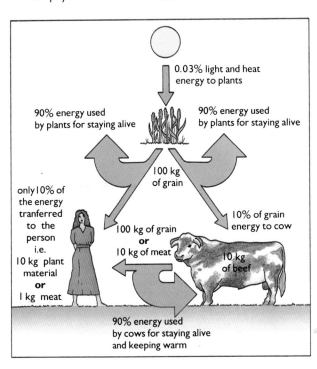

Losing energy?

In an energy chain, energy is converted from one form to another at each stage. But not *all* the energy gets converted to the useful end product—some is converted to other things along the way.

EXPLORE
- How much useful energy passes from the plants to the cow?
- Where does the rest of the energy go?
- How much useful energy passes from the cow to the person?
- Where does the rest go?
- How much useful energy passes from the plants to the person if the person eats grain?

Efficient lighting

These diagrams show two sorts of lights.

EXPLORE
- Which type of light gives the most useful energy?
- Which light would you use in a room where it was important not to heat up the room?
- Write an energy chain for each type of light showing where the energy goes to.

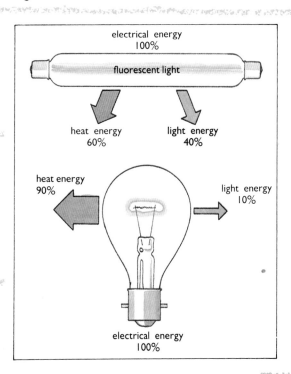

WATERWORKS!

We can all enjoy and use our rivers. But maintaining them must be top priority so that others can use them too.

EXPLORE

- How is this river being used?
- Which do you think are good uses and which are bad uses? Why?
- How are the uses causing pollution to the river? Make a table like this.

If the use is an **observation** underline it in green. If it is an **inference**, underline it in red.

How is the river being used?	Does it cause pollution?	What is the effect of this pollution?
The sewage works use it to get rid of waste	Yes - phosphates	Phosphates make algae grow quickly which reduces oxygen.

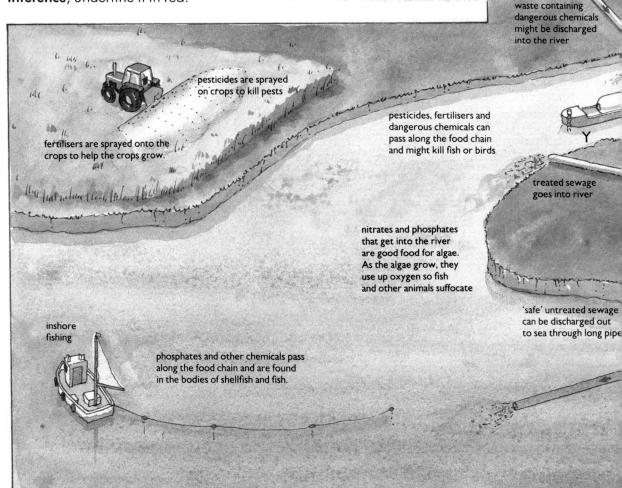

many factories cau[se] air pollution which can produce acid r[ain]

factories use a lot of water to make their products

waste containing dangerous chemicals might be discharged into the river

pesticides are sprayed on crops to kill pests

fertilisers are sprayed onto the crops to help the crops grow.

pesticides, fertilisers and dangerous chemicals can pass along the food chain and might kill fish or birds

treated sewage goes into river

nitrates and phosphates that get into the river are good food for algae. As the algae grow, they use up oxygen so fish and other animals suffocate

'safe' untreated sewage can be discharged out to sea through long pipe[s]

inshore fishing

phosphates and other chemicals pass along the food chain and are found in the bodies of shellfish and fish.

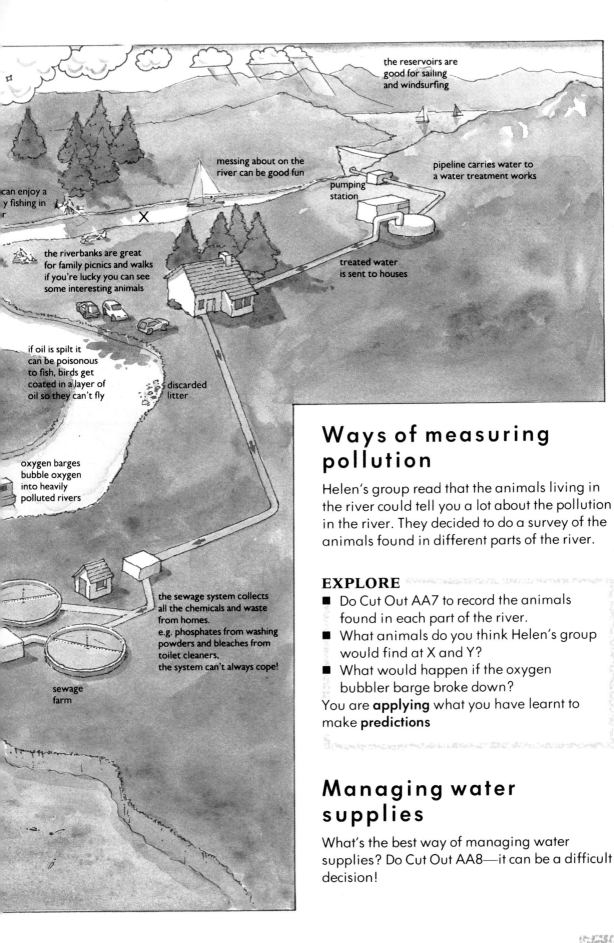

the reservoirs are good for sailing and windsurfing

messing about on the river can be good fun

pipeline carries water to a water treatment works

pumping station

can enjoy a y fishing in r

X

the riverbanks are great for family picnics and walks if you're lucky you can see some interesting animals

treated water is sent to houses

if oil is spilt it can be poisonous to fish, birds get coated in a layer of oil so they can't fly

discarded litter

oxygen barges bubble oxygen into heavily polluted rivers

the sewage system collects all the chemicals and waste from homes. e.g. phosphates from washing powders and bleaches from toilet cleaners, the system can't always cope!

sewage farm

Ways of measuring pollution

Helen's group read that the animals living in the river could tell you a lot about the pollution in the river. They decided to do a survey of the animals found in different parts of the river.

EXPLORE
- Do Cut Out AA7 to record the animals found in each part of the river.
- What animals do you think Helen's group would find at X and Y?
- What would happen if the oxygen bubbler barge broke down?

You are **applying** what you have learnt to make **predictions**

Managing water supplies

What's the best way of managing water supplies? Do Cut Out AA8—it can be a difficult decision!

WEATHER AND WIND

Shock hurricane wrecks countryside
oct '89

Phew wotta scorcha!
July 89

South westerly winds bring flash floods

Temperatures drop to −5°C as easterlies bring icy cold weather

What other weather headlines can you remember? Make a list and note why you remember them, and what you were doing that day.

In Britain there is different weather when different **airstreams** move over the country.

EXPLORE
- Which months of the year do you think Easterly airstreams are common?
- Why do you think the South Westerlies that have moved over Europe bring little rain? You are **interpreting**.

airstreams from the southwest bring warm wet weather if they move over the Atlantic

airstreams from the east bring cold dry weather
Moscow

Atlantic Ocean

airstreams from the southwest bring warm dry weather if they move over Europe

Paris
Madrid
Rome

Britain has weather that often changes quite suddenly. This happens when different airstreams meet.

EXPLORE
- **Record** how the different airstreams cause different types of weather. Use Cut Out AA9 (Part 1) to help you.

We get clear, hot sticky summer days when a warm moist airstream is moving over

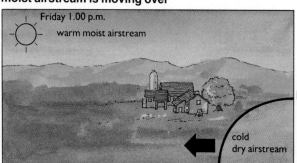

Friday 1.00 p.m.
warm moist airstream
cold dry airstream

But there can then suddenly be heavy rain or thunderstorms

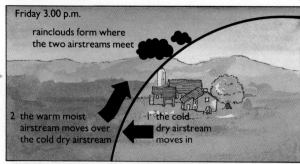

Friday 3.00 p.m.
rainclouds form where the two airstreams meet
2 the warm moist airstream moves over the cold dry airstream
1 the cold dry airstream moves in

We get clear, cold winter days when a cold dry airstream is moving over

Tuesday 10.00 a.m.
dry cold airstream
moist warm airstream

But this can quickly change to dull, drizzly weather

Tuesday 12.00 noon
rainclouds form where the two airstreams meet
dry cold airstream
moist warm airstream moves over the cold dry airstream

3.14

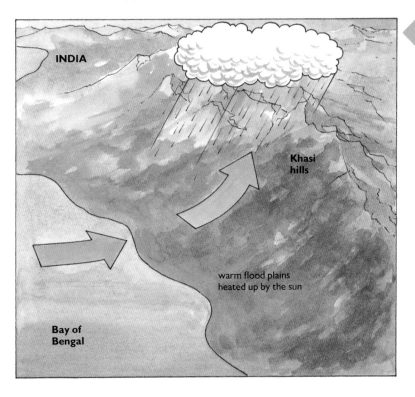

Monsoons are airstreams that move in the same pattern every year. They can be **predicted**.

The monsoons bring rain to Bangladesh at the same time every year. Warm moist airstreams move over the sea. The airstreams get warmer and rise up when they move over the flood plains. They rise up quickly when they reach the Khasi hills and make huge rain clouds. The rainfalls are very heavy—up to 1000 cm per year.

EXPLORE
- Use this information to label the diagram on Cut Out AA9 (Part 2). You are **interpreting**.

This part of Sundar Ali's diary explains how his family in Bangladesh plant their crops ready for the rainfall.

EXPLORE
- Record which statements are **observations**, **inferences**, **hypotheses** and **predictions**.

Thousands drowned in floods

80% of Bangladesh is now under water following the floods which have engulfed the low-lying land. Thousands of people have been drowned and millions are homeless as crops, livestock and homes were washed away in the torrent.

Some people were lucky to scramble to the roofs of houses or the tops of hills but face a bleak future when the floods subside. The health authorities have already warned that diseases such as cholera and dysentry will be a major problem as well as the malnutrition resulting from lack of food.

Sundar's diary

April 22nd 1988   A busy week, we've weeded the fields-my back hurts! Spent 2 days repairing the roof – the monsoon rain will never get in now!

May 11th 1988 Finished planting the rice. Father put down fertilizer first - it cost a fortune but he said we must get a good crop this year. We planted extra tomatoes and beans.
Picked our first ripe pineapple today. The crop looks good - we should be able to sell a lot. The mangoes are HUGE - they'll be ready next week.

June 8th 1988 It's hot and the clouds are grey and huge. I think the monsoon will start in a few days. I hope the rains are good. The chickens are getting fat.

In 1988 monsoons brought torrential rain which flooded the crops.

EXPLORE
- List the ways that you think Sundar Ali's family were affected by the floods. You are **interpreting**.
- What other things beside the monsoons could have caused the floods? These are your **inferences**.

WEATHER SYMBOLS

Nice day?

People in the UK talk about the weather a lot. They are often very interested in the weather forecast. Why do you think this is?

Here is a newspaper weather forecast for Saturday 21 May 1990.

EXPLORE

Here are some weather symbols.

- How many of each symbol can you find on the map?
- Write a sentence about the kind of weather shown by each symbol. These words might help you:

    sunny, windy, cloudy, patchy, rainy, heavy

- What do you think the symbol means?
- What do you think the symbol ④ means?

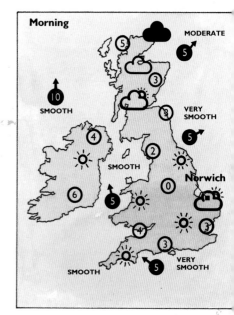

Nice evening?

These are the weather maps for the afternoon and night of Saturday 21 May 1990.

EXPLORE
- What extra symbol is there on these maps?
- What do you think it stands for?
- Mark lives in the city of Norwich, which is marked on the map. Mark keeps a weather diary, and the page for Saturday 21 May 1990 is shown below. The gaps are where his dog chewed his diary. Rewrite his diary for him filling in the gaps.

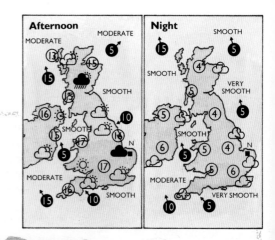

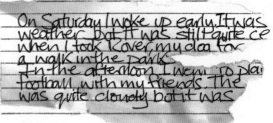

On Saturday I woke up early. It was _____ weather but it was still quite ce _____ when I took Rover, my dog, for a walk in the park. _____ In the afternoon I went to play football with my friends. The _____ was quite cloudy but it was _____

More maps

Here are some more weather maps for Norwich on 21 May 1990.

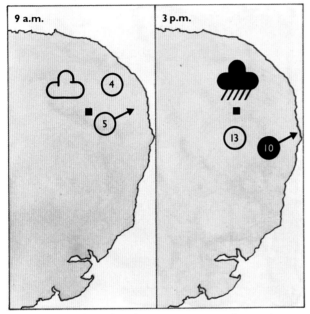

Weather map from local newspaper morning and evening editions

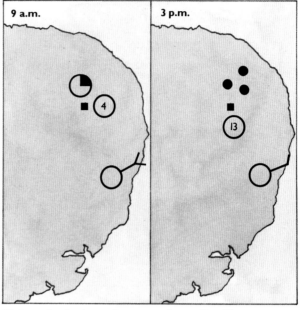

Meteorological map from coastguard's office

EXPLORE

- Copy the signs used on the meteorological map.
- Match them to the signs meaning the same thing in the newspaper report.
- Write a description for each sign.
- Make newspaper and meteorological maps for this radio weather report from Norwich at 6 p.m. on 21 May 1990.

> The weather is patchy. It is getting cool quite quickly. At present it is 8°C and the winds are quite strong at 12 knots. It has stopped raining but it is cloudy and dull.

PRESENT

- Make a diary of the weather in your area for 12 hours— at 9 a.m., 12 noon, 3 p.m., 6 p.m. and 9 p.m.
- Compare it with the newspaper reports that morning. How accurate are the reports?
- Make a plan of a textbook page that shows a newspaper and a meteorological weather map for that day using the symbols you have learnt.

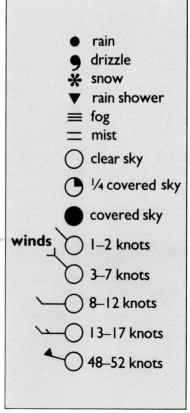

▲ **More meteorological signs**

WHY THINGS MOVE

Forcing a move

EXPLORE

- How could you make these balls move? Make a list.
- How could you stop them once they were moving? Make a list.

The lists you have made are lists of **forces**. To make something move or to stop it moving you use a force. Forces are measured in **newtons** (N), named after Isaac Newton who studied forces in the seventeenth century.

▶ Keeping things still

There are forces involved here as well, even though nothing is moving.

The two girls are the same weight (weight is a force). The girl on the right has sunk into the snow, because it cannot support her weight. The girl on the left is wearing skis. These spread the force over a greater area, so there is more snow to support her weight.

EXPLORE

- Use the idea of forces spreading out to explain what is happening in the pictures of the drawing pin.

Under pressure

Pressure is used to describe the idea of forces spreading out.

Pressure is worked out by dividing the size of the force by the area it is spread over:

$$\text{pressure} = \frac{\text{force}}{\text{area}}$$

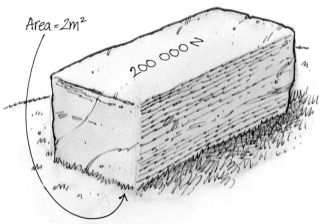

Area = 2m²

200 000 N

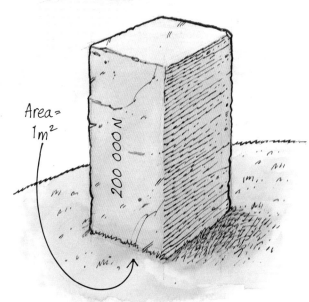

Area = 1m²

200 000 N

Pressure = $\frac{\text{force}}{\text{area}}$

= $\frac{200\ 000}{2}$

= 100 000 N/m²

In the top picture, a lump of concrete weighing 200 000 N is lying on a piece of ground with an area of 2 square metres. In the second picture, the concrete is standing on its end, so it only presses on 1 square metre of ground. Which way round will the concrete make the deepest dent in the ground?

Pressure = $\frac{\text{force}}{\text{area}}$

= $\frac{200\ 000}{1}$

= 100 000 N/m²

EXPLORE

■ Use the idea of pressure to explain why:
(a) it is easier to cut butter with a knife than a spoon
(b) camels can walk more easily than horses over soft sand
(c) you need special tyres on a motorbike to ride over muddy fields.

■ Think of some other **applications** of pressure in everyday life.

BEE SCIENTIFIC

A sting in the tail

Do you panic if a bee comes near you? There are over 200 types of bee in the UK which can all sting, but they don't unless they're attacked.

Did you know that bees are insects?

And insects are animals, so bees are animals.

Bumble bee

Queen (in centre) and drone honey bees

Wool-carder bee

Leafcutter bee

grasshopper

butterfly

stag beetle

dragonfly

lady bird

cow

geranium

starfish

oak tree

rhinocerous

EXPLORE

- The pictures show some different types of bee.
  What differences can you **observe** between these bees?
- These diagrams show some other insects. What similarities can you **observe** between bees and these insects? Cut Out LS1 (Part 1) will help.
- These diagrams show some other living things. What do you think bees have in common with these organisms? Cut Out LS1 (Part 1) will help.

Let's bee social, honey!

Honey bees are social insects—they live in large organised groups. Each bee has a role to play to help the group survive.

There are three types of honey bee. The **queen** and the **drones** reproduce to keep up the supply of new bees. **Workers** feed and care for the group. There may be 60 000 workers in a group.

What do bees eat?

Worker bees collect **nectar**, a sugary liquid produced by plants. They take the nectar into their stomachs, then regurgitate it and convert it into honey when they return to the hive.

I'll feed you if you pollinate me . . .

The plants get something in return for feeding bees. Plants produce **pollen** on structures called **stamens**. Pollen is like a powder, and it contains the plant's male sex cells. When bees collect nectar from flowers, their legs brush against the stamens and pollen sticks to them. When they visit another flower, some pollen falls off and lands on the **carpels**—which contain the plant's female sex cells. Fertilisation only happens between pollen from one flower and carpels from another, so bees help plants to reproduce sexually.

Why do bees behive the way they do?

One worker bee cannot carry much nectar on its own, so when it finds a good plant it 'tells' the rest of the group. Bees communicate by **dancing**—they move around the hive in simple patterns which show where the food is. Worker bees perform two dances. One is called the **round dance** which shows how far away the food supply is. The other is called the **waggle dance** and shows the direction of the food.

Round dance—the bee flies quickly in one direction and then in the other. This means that the food is within 100 metres. The more circles in the dance, the further away the food is. If it is more than 100m away, the bee does a waggle dance

This worker bee will transfer pollen from this flower to the next one it visits

PRESENT

- Draw a strip cartoon to show a young child how bees collect nectar and pollinate flowers at the same time.

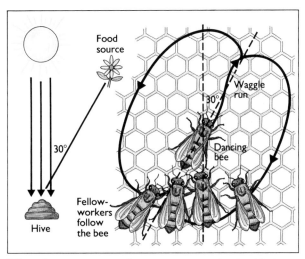

Waggle dance—the bee moves round a double loop, with a straight line between the loops. The bee waggles her body on the straight part of the dance. The waggling sends scent from the flowers to the other bees.
The straight line also shows the direction of the flowers. If it goes straight up the hive, then the flowers can be found by flying towards the Sun. If it is at an angle of 30° to the hive, then the flowers are on a path 30° to the Sun

EXPLORE

- **Interpret** bees' dances. Cut Out LS1 (Part 2) gives some dances.

PRESENT

- What other useful information might bees communicate? Write a story for a wildlife magazine imagining you are a bee trying to communicate with other bees in a hive.

BENDING LIGHT

You can see the words on this page because they reflect light. The light reflected from the words travels to your eye in a straight line.

Have you ever seen words **on a page** made to look different by a lens? What do you think lenses do to light?

lens

light box

focal point

focal length

A lens that makes light bend together and meet at one point is called a **convex lens**. A thick convex lens bends light more than a thin convex lens.

When light goes into a lens and comes out the other side its direction changes. The lens bends the light

Eye see

EXPLORE
- Use a whole page to copy this picture of the eye and label it. Use Cut Out LS2 (Part 1) to help you.

Your eye uses its **cornea** and **lens** to bend the light that comes into it. The muscles of the iris change the size of the pupil. This controls the amount of light entering the eye. The **ciliary muscles** can change the shape of the lens to focus the light. The light then travels through the liquid in your eye and falls on the **retina** at the back. Here there is a layer of cells which are sensitive to light. The cells pick up messages from the light. The **optic nerve** carries these messages to the brain.

EXPLORE
- Add labels to your diagram of the eye showing the function of each part. Cut Out LS2 (Part 2) will help you. You are **interpreting**.

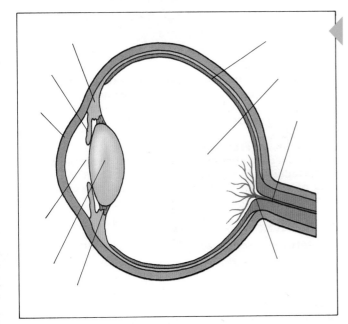

Clear as mud?

Not everyone has perfect eyesight. The light coming into the eye may be bent too much or too little—it doesn't focus on the retina.

People with 'short sight' see things that are close to them clearly but this is how they see things that are in the distance. ▼

People with 'long sight' see things in the distance clearly but this is how they see things that are close to them. ▼

▼

This is because the eyeball is longer than normal so light from things in the distance is focused in front of the retina.

▼

This is because the eyeball is shorter than normal so light from an object close to the eye is focused behind the retina.

PRESENT

- Make a poster for an optician's waiting-room showing how long-sighted and short-sighted people focus light. Cut Out LS3 (Part 1) will help you.

This camera works in a similar way to the eye except that the lens is in front of the aperture. It takes light in through the **aperture**, focuses it with a **lens** and lets the picture fall on the **film**.

▼

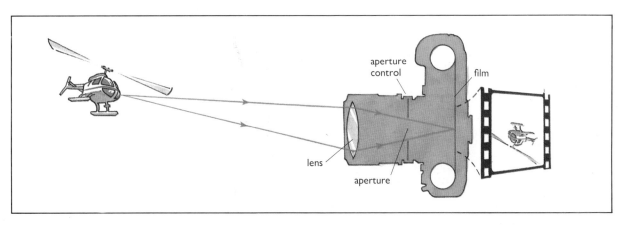

EXPLORE

- Make a table to compare the parts of the eye and the parts of the camera which work in a similar way. Use Cut Out LS3 (Part 2) to help you.

BETTER SOUND

EXPLORE

- Have you got any records or tapes that were digitally recorded?
- Do a survey of records and tapes to find how many are digitally recorded.
- Ask some people if they think digital recording is better than other methods, and if so why.

Golden oldies

The first record players used records that revolved 78 times per minute (78 r.p.m.). The records had grooves with bumps and hollows along them which were similar or **analogous** to sound waves. As the needle went along the groove, it moved sideways over the bumps. This movement was converted into sound signals which the horn **amplified** (made louder).

The 78 r.p.m. records were big and heavy and easily scratched. Present-day **analogue** records work in the same way.

The grooves of an LP have sideways bumps which move the needle

EXPLORE

- List three things that can go wrong with this system.
- Give three reasons why you might buy an analogue record.

Compact discs

Technology has come a long way since 78s, but even music from modern LPs is slightly distorted by hiss and crackles. Compact discs do not have this problem. They do not have grooves that are read by a needle — they have bumpy surfaces that are read by a laser beam. The laser beam does not wear or scratch the surface.

Dig it all

The music on compact discs is recorded and played **digitally**. The bumps on the surface of the disc cause a '1' to go to the computer, the pits cause a '0' to go to the computer. The pattern of sound will be a mixture of '0's and '1's. This mixture is called a **binary code**. You may have come across binary codes in maths.

EXPLORE

The binary code represented in the top diagram is 1010 1100 and is part of a note.
- Draw a compact disc surface that represents the following binary codes:
  - 1100 1101
  - 0100 0011
  - 1110 0110
- Underneath each drawing show whether the laser beam will be reflected or not by writing 'on' or 'off'.

Binary codes are used in digital recording. Music is recorded by a computer as a series of '1's and '0's. When the digits are played back, the sound produced is almost exactly the same as the original.

EXPLORE
- List three advantages of digital recording and playing.
- Look back at the disadvantages of analogue records. Which ones do compact discs overcome?
- What disadvantages do compact discs have?

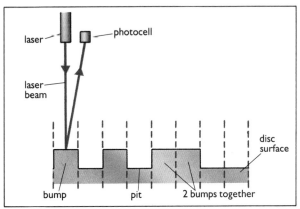

A compact disc is made up of bumps and pits. A laser beam is shone at the disc and is reflected from the bumps, but not from the pits.

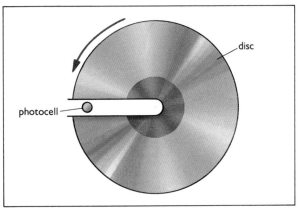

As the disc spins round, a photocell detects whether the laser is reflected or not at any instant.

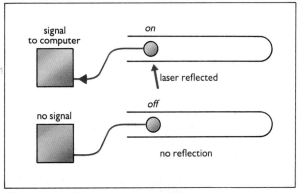

The photocell switches an electrical signal *on* each time the laser is reflected, and *off* each time it is not reflected. The pattern made by these electrical signals is interpreted by a computer and turned into very high quality sound.

PRESENT
- Design an advertisement to tell people about digital sound, and to explain why it is better than analogue sound.

COMMUNICATIONS SATELLITES

Straight around the world

In 1901, an Italian scientist called Guglielmo Marconi sent a radio message across the Atlantic Ocean—almost one-tenth of the Earth's circumference. Radio waves travel in straight lines and the Earth is curved, so why didn't the waves go straight off into space?

About a year later, Oliver Heaviside **predicted** that the radio waves were reflected back by a special layer in the Earth's atmosphere. Once people started investigating this **hypothesis** the layer was soon found. It was named the Heaviside layer after him.

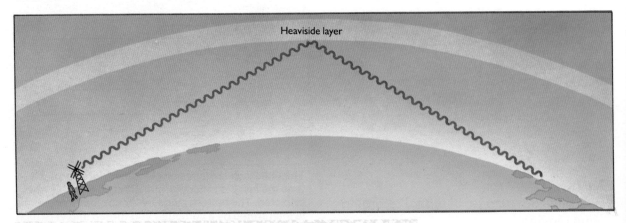

PRESENT

■ Write a radio play about the history of long-distance communication. You can include as many characters as you like.
Act 1 should include what Marconi thought and found out.
Act 2 should be about the Heaviside layer.

The Heaviside layer often fades away, so it is not a very reliable way of reflecting radio waves. One idea for overcoming this was to produce an artificial reflector. This was a huge balloon, 30 metres across, covered in aluminium to make it reflect better.

EXPLORE

■ The first balloon launched to reflect radio waves was called *Echo 1*. Why do you think it had this name?

■ Draw a cartoon to show how this balloon worked.

Satellites — communication breakthrough

Satellites are even better than balloons. They do not just reflect the radio waves — they have equipment to receive waves, make them bigger and then direct them towards their target.

Satellites can be placed very precisely above the Earth. A satellite placed about 40 000 km up will orbit the Earth every 24 hours. As the Earth spins round once every 24 hours the satellite stays above one place on the Earth's surface — so it is always available for use there.

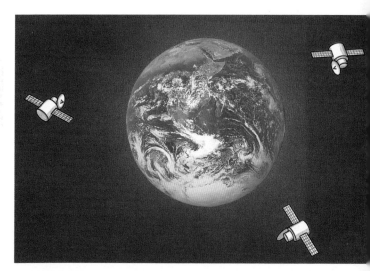

This satellite handles telephone, data, radio and television signals

PRESENT

■ Add another act to your play to include balloons and satellites.

What else do satellites do?

Satellites are used for other things beside radio. Television and other types of communications use satellites a great deal. People use satellites that move slowly around the Earth to follow weather systems, such as hurricanes, so they can predict the weather more accurately. Satellites are also used to map the Earth accurately, or to follow changes in snow cover or forest growth. These are known as Earth resource satellites. Probably the largest use of satellites is by military organisations, which use them for spying on other countries. There are plans to develop satellites as mobile weapons platforms to attack other countries.

Three satellites can provide communications all over the Earth

PRESENT

■ Finish your play with acts 4 and 5. Act 4 should be about uses of satellites now. Act 5 is about the future — how will satellites be used in 30 years' time? For peaceful purposes or for hostile purposes?

HOW WE USE ELECTROMAGNETS

What is electromagnetism?

Penny's group were revising what they had learnt about electromagnetism.

EXPLORE
- **Record** the ideas you agree with.
- Add anything else your group knows about electromagnetism.

Electromagnets are made of a coil of wire around a piece of iron.

Electromagnets can be made of any metal.

You need a coil of wire to make an electromagnet.

Loudspeakers, electric bells, telephones and tape recorders, all have electromagnets to make them work.

Ringing the doorbell

Penny never knew when any of her friends called because the doorbell didn't work! She found these two pictures which show what should happen when someone rings the doorbell.

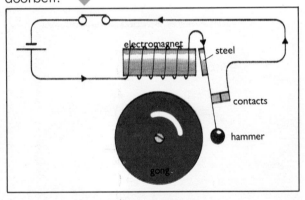

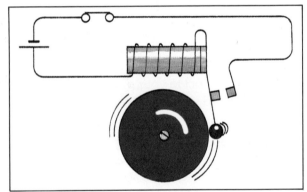

EXPLORE
- The electromagnet inside the bell switches itself on and off very quickly. Make a flick book to show how the electric bell works. Use Cut Out LS4.
- **Record** what happens when someone presses a doorbell. Use these sentences to help you. Add other information from the pictures or your flick book.

- This continues until the person stops pressing the doorbell
- This demagnetises the electromagnet and makes the hammer spring back towards the contacts
- As soon as the contacts meet, the electric circuit is complete and the process starts again
- The movement of the steel and hammer pulls the contacts apart and breaks the electric circuit
- First the electricity flows through the contacts and the coil of wire
- This magnetises the electromagnet so the piece of steel is attracted to the electromagnet
- This makes the hammer hit the gong and make a sound

Penny's group discussed how they could put the bell back together so that it would ring more loudly. These were their **hypotheses**.

EXPLORE
- **Record** the ones you agree with.
- What other **hypotheses** does your group have?

How do loudspeakers work?

The loudspeaker in a radio or record player changes electrical energy into sound energy. It does this by vibrating its cone forwards and backwards very quickly.

EXPLORE
- Read the descriptions of the parts of the loudspeaker.
  Use them to label the loudspeaker diagram on Cut Out LS5 (Part 1). You are **interpreting**.

  - There is a **metal frame** outside the cone
  - The inside of the **cone** is made of stiff paper. It is 10 cm in diameter
  - The **permanent magnet** is at the back of the cone. It is grey
  - The **coil** is 2 cm long and made of copper wire
  - The **supports** are made of thin metal. They join the metal frame and paper part of the cone

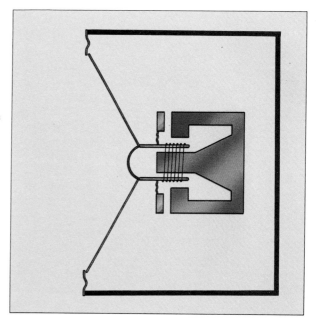

PRESENT
- A hi-fi company want to put a leaflet with their loudspeaker to show customers how they work. Make a flow chart for the leaflet. Use Cut Out LS5 (Part 2) to help you.

MUSICAL INSTRUMENTS

The shape of notes to come

Ruth and Jeremiah were looking at the patterns made by their voices on an oscilloscope.

'They're different even when we say the same things', **observed** Ruth.

'Even when we sing the same notes', **observed** Jeremiah.

'The patterns have the same basic shape', Ruth went on.

'It's the bumps on them that are different', said Jeremiah.

'Perhaps that's how we can tell different voices apart', suggested Ruth.

'Yes', said Jeremiah. 'It might also be the way we can tell one musical instrument from another.'

'Let's try and collect some patterns of different instruments playing the same note', said Ruth.

EXPLORE
- What variable are Ruth and Jeremiah **investigating**?
- What factor are they controlling?

Instrumental patterns

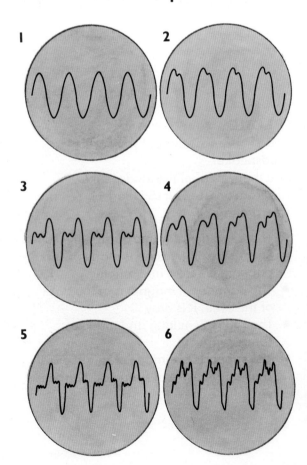

Note the quality

A pure note has a smooth wave pattern without any bumps on it. A glockenspiel is one instrument which produces this sort of pattern.

The little bumps on some wave patterns are called harmonics. They give a sound its quality. A violin has a large number of harmonics, both before and after the main note. A piano has only one harmonic, which happens after the main note. Trumpets, horns and clarinets have harmonics before the main note, although the clarinet has a few afterwards as well. The trumpet and the horn have rather similar patterns, which might be expected as they are similar types of instrument. However, the harmonics on the horn make less difference to the main note than the harmonics on the trumpet. People describe the sound of the horn as a mellow note, and the trumpet as a sharp note.

PRESENT
- You have just invented a machine which tells who people are by their voices — a 'voiceprint' machine. Make a poster explaining how it works to persuade your local police station to buy one.

NOTES

Playing the guitar

Guitars only have six strings, but guitarists can make lots of notes. How do they do this? There are three main ways to make a note higher on a guitar.

Use a thin string ▶

▼ **Make the string shorter**

Picture the sound

If you make a note into an oscilloscope you can see a picture of each note.

The number of waves each second is called the frequency of the note.

EXPLORE

- Do you have more or fewer waves each second for a high note?
- Which has the higher frequency, a low note or a high note?
- Draw a diagram of the picture you would get on an oscilloscope for a medium note. You are **predicting**.

Tighten a string ▲

EXPLORE

- How do you think you would make a note lower on a guitar?
- Name some other stringed instruments you know.
- How do you make a note lower on those instruments?
- How do you think you could get the same note using two different sized strings?

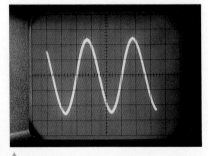

▲
Oscilloscope picture of a low note

◀ **Oscilloscope picture of a high note**

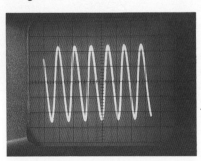

Piano or forte?

Here is another oscilloscope picture, showing the same note played quietly and loudly ▼

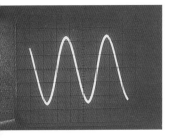 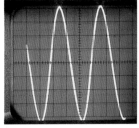

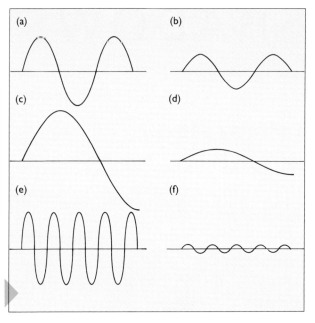

(a)   (b)   (c)   (d)   (e)   (f)

EXPLORE

- How do you know it is the same note?
  You are **applying**.
- Which note do you think is quieter?
  You are **predicting**.
- Look at these diagrams of different notes.
  For each diagram decide whether it is a
  high, low or medium note and whether it
  was played loudly or softly. You are
  applying.

Making music

EXPLORE

You have inherited a violin but all the
strings are broken. It should have four
different strings but you only have two
medium sized strings and two thin strings.
- How could you use these strings to make
  four different notes on the violin?

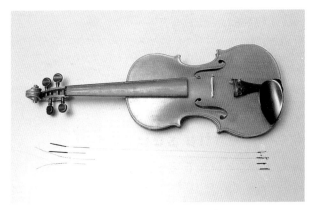

PRESENT

Delia made this makeshift double bass. It
worked but its notes were too high and too
quiet.
- Draw a diagram showing her how to
  make the sound lower and louder.

SHADOWS

A shady story

More than anything he hated having to walk across the graveyard at night. It frightened him. There was the rustling of the trees, the creaking of the branches and the wind whistling through the alleys. He felt fine once he got up by the church wall. There was a light on the other side, but tonight it made shadows all around the church hall. Suddenly there was a crash—something moved in the shadow........

EXPLORE
- What times of day do you notice shadows most?
- How do you think shadows are formed?

You have probably seen shadows like these

> You get lots of shadows when there's lots of light.

> The light should be weak.

> You need the Sun to make a shadow.

> You get shadows at night as well as during the day.

> Shadows are made on flat surfaces like walls and floors.

> Buildings and trees get in the way of the Sun, that's when you get shadows.

> You need little things in the way of a light to make a shadow.

EXPLORE
Giovanna's group discussed the pictures and had these ideas about how shadows are made.
- Which ones do you agree with?
- Write down the ideas you agree with. Add your own ideas.

4.8

Looking at shadows

Giovanna's group tested their ideas using a shadow puppet they'd made in a technology lesson. Each time they made a shadow they drew around the shape they got.

They shone a light and held the puppet close to the screen

They held it a long way from the screen

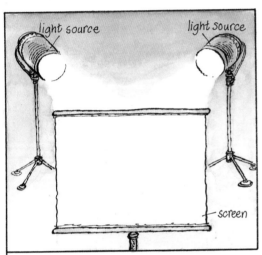

They used two lights from different places

EXPLORE

Giovanna's group's results are shown on Cut Out LS7 (Part 1).

■ Match the descriptions to the drawings on the Cut Out.

Giovanna's group also drew around the shadows and measured the distance from the puppet. Their drawings are on Cut Out LS7 (Part 2).

■ Complete their drawings using the Cut Out.

To puppet you in the picture

Giovanna's group discussed their puppet work.

EXPLORE

■ Use their ideas to make your own statements about how puppets make shadows. Add your own ideas as well.

■ Draw a diagram of a bulb, a puppet and a screen. Write on it how shadows are made.

PRESENT

■ Design a puppet theatre to perform a puppet play that would teach younger childen how shadows are made.

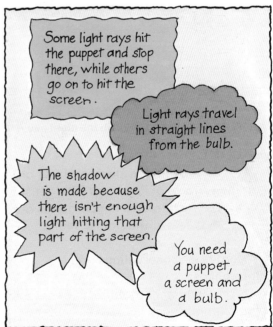

Some light rays hit the puppet and stop there, while others go on to hit the screen.

Light rays travel in straight lines from the bulb.

The shadow is made because there isn't enough light hitting that part of the screen.

You need a puppet, a screen and a bulb.

STARS

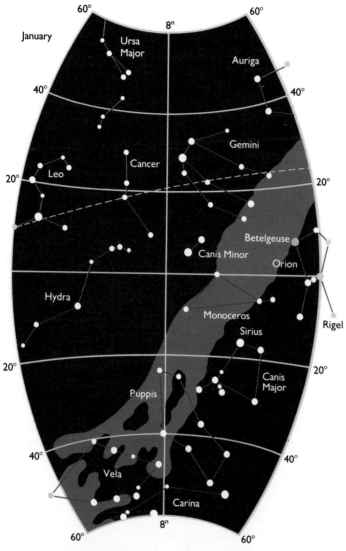

Use this star map to find Orion in the night sky

EXPLORE

- What do you think the temperatures are on the surfaces of Rigel and Betelgeuse?
- What do you think the temperatures are on the surfaces of the stars in the diagram? ▶
- **Record** these **observations** and **inferences**.
- Find out where these stars can be seen in the night sky.

Seeing stars

Have you ever noticed that stars are not all the same colour? You may have to look hard, but a good place to start is with the group of stars called **Orion**. Betelgeuse is a dull red star, while Rigel is a very bright star with a blue colour in its light.

Astronomers (people who study the stars) have **observed** the colours of thousands of stars. They have used their observations to make **inferences** about the temperatures of stars, by using this information:

Colour	Temperature
Blue	Over 25 000 °C
White	8000–10 000 °C
Yellow	5000–7500 °C
Orange	4000–5000 °C
Red	3000–4000 °C

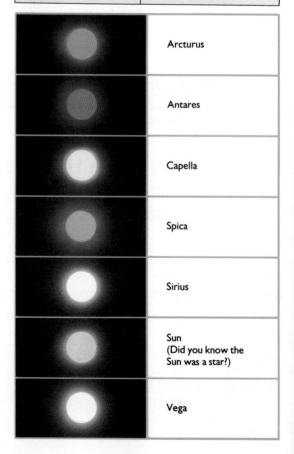

	Arcturus
	Antares
	Capella
	Spica
	Sirius
	Sun (Did you know the Sun was a star?)
	Vega

Star groups

Two astronomers, Annie Cannon and Wilhelmina Fleming, **classified** their observations of star colour. They named each group after a letter of the alphabet.

This classification helps us **interpret** changes in the universe that happen over a long period of time.

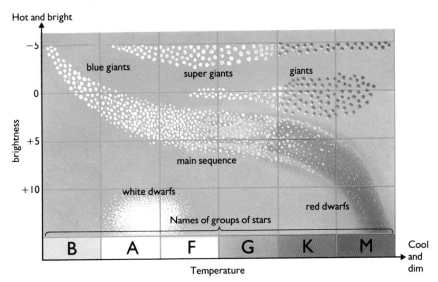

The life of stars

Stars start life as clouds of dust which are gradually forced together by gravity. As they get nearer they heat up until the temperature is high enough for nuclear reactions to start. These nuclear reactions in stars convert hydrogen into helium. This produces energy, which is very useful to us—the energy that reaches Earth comes from the conversion of hydrogen to helium in the Sun. Stars which are producing energy like this are described as being on the **main sequence**. Exactly where they are on the diagram depends on how big they are and how much hydrogen they have used up. Most stars are on the main sequence. When a star has used up all its hydrogen fuel it expands and becomes a 'red giant' star. It uses up all the other types of fuel it has, and then explodes and forms a 'white dwarf' star.

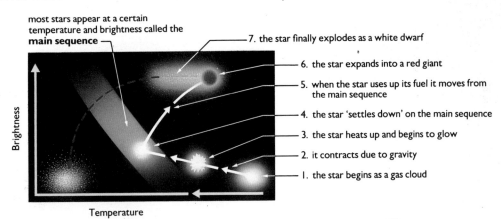

most stars appear at a certain temperature and brightness called the **main sequence**

7. the star finally explodes as a white dwarf
6. the star expands into a red giant
5. when the star uses up its fuel it moves from the main sequence
4. the star 'settles down' on the main sequence
3. the star heats up and begins to glow
2. it contracts due to gravity
1. the star begins as a gas cloud

When a star has used up all its hydrogen fuel it expands and becomes a 'red giant' star. It uses up all the other types of fuel it has, and then explodes and forms a 'white dwarf' star.

The life of a star—astronomers think these changes are going on all the time, so there are stars at each stage all over the universe

PRESENT
- Collect pictures and make a poster to get people interested in astronomy, showing the changes that happen to stars, *or*
- Write a 'life history' of a star for an astronomy magazine, from a cloud of gas to a white dwarf.

SUMMER TIME

Lots of things on the Earth change, but one thing everyone is certain about is that it will get dark tonight, and light again in the morning. Why does this happen? Here are some ideas about what happens at night.

EXPLORE

- Do you agree with any of these ideas?
- What do you think causes day and night? **Record** some of your ideas.

From darkness to light

Every 24 hours the Earth spins around once. We say it rotates on its own axis. Because of this, at any one time half the world is in daylight while the other half is in darkness. There is also a time between daylight and darkness in the morning called dawn, and one in the evening called dusk.

The Earth spins on its axis (A), and also moves around the Sun (B)

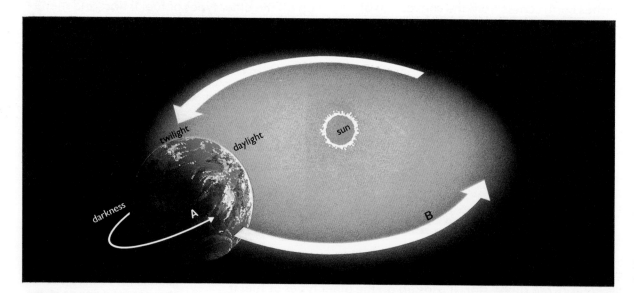

twilight
daylight
sun
darkness
A
B

EXPLORE

- Why do you think it is midday in New Zealand when it is midnight in the UK?
- Where is the Sun when it is midnight in the UK?
- In the UK, are shadows longer in the winter or summer? Why do you think there is a difference?

PRESENT

- Draw a diagram of the Earth and the Sun for a travel agent's brochure that shows why it's 8 p.m. in Greece when it's 6 p.m. in the UK.

What time is it?

If you want to telephone someone in another country, you need to know what time it is there to avoid getting him or her out of bed. To work out time differences we have divided the world into **time zones**.

EXPLORE

- What time is it in Washington when it's midnight in the UK?
- What time is it in Kinshasa when it's midday in the UK?
- What time is it in the UK when it's 9 a.m. in Seoul?
- If it takes five hours to fly to Cairo and you left the UK at 10 a.m., what time would it be in Cairo when you arrived?
- At 2300 hours (GMT) people in the UK saw a live broadcast of a golf match at 1800 hours local time. What country could the golf course be in?

This map of the Earth shows the international time zones

What causes the seasons?

The Earth is tilted on its path around the Sun. This causes the seasons throughout the year— the Earth travels around the Sun once in a year

PRESENT

- Use Cut Out LS8 to make a sundial. Set up the sundial so that the pointer points due South. **Predict** where the shadow will fall on the dial at different times.

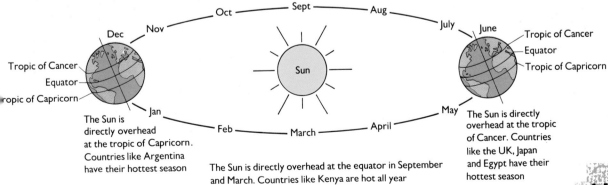

Tropic of Cancer
Equator
Tropic of Capricorn

The Sun is directly overhead at the tropic of Capricorn. Countries like Argentina have their hottest season

The Sun is directly overhead at the equator in September and March. Countries like Kenya are hot all year

Tropic of Cancer
Equator
Tropic of Capricorn

The Sun is directly overhead at the tropic of Cancer. Countries like the UK, Japan and Egypt have their hottest season

4.10

THE MOON

People have been fascinated by the Moon for thousands of years. Below are some ideas about the Moon.

EXPLORE

- What can you **observe** about the Moon?
- How do you think the shapes on the Moon were formed?

There's a man on the Moon that comes out sometimes.

The moon looks after you at night.

It's made of cheese. You can see the holes in it.

?

The Moon's cycle

The Moon takes 29.5 days to go around the Earth. It also spins around on its axis every 29.5 days, so the same side of the Moon faces us all the time. The Moon doesn't produce its own light—it reflects sunlight. As the Sun is a star it produces its own light.

Only the part of the Moon facing the Sun gets lit up, so the shape we can see changes over the 29.5-day cycle. Light takes 1.3 seconds to reach planet Earth from the Moon, but takes 8.3 minutes to reach our planet from the Sun. Why do you think this is?

First quarter—8 days into the cycle

Full Moon—14 days

Final crescent—27 days

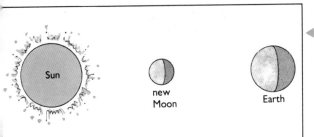

When the Moon is between the Sun and the Earth it cannot be seen—this is called a new Moon

When the Earth is between the Sun and the Moon the full reflection can be seen—this is called a full Moon

All the other shapes you can see depend upon the area of the reflected light that a person on Earth can see

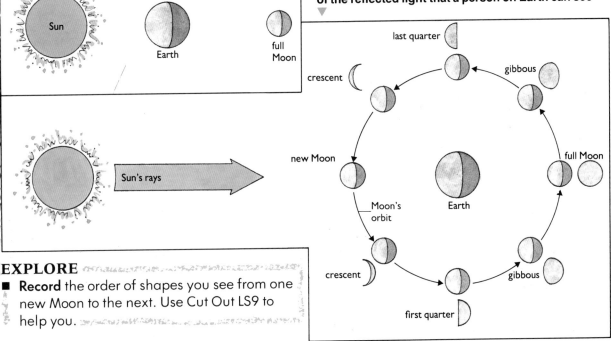

EXPLORE
- **Record** the order of shapes you see from one new Moon to the next. Use Cut Out LS9 to help you.

How does the Moon affect us?

People have always paid a lot of attention to the Moon's cycle. Farmers relied on it to tell them when to plant their crops and when to harvest them. Some religious festivals are determined by the Moon.

EXPLORE
- Can you think of a religious festival which depends on the Moon?
- Find out how long the year is in a lunar calendar. (Use reference books to help you.)
- Look at the calendar you use in school. Is it based on the Moon?
- How long is the year used in your school calendar?
- Is this the same as the year used in a lunar calendar?
- Can you think of another natural cycle that takes the same time as the Moon's? Do you think this is just coincidence?

THE STORY OF RADIO

1864

Hi, I'm Maxwell. James Maxwell. I've just worked out some equations. From these I predict that electricity makes invisible waves.

That's silly! If they're invisible how's anyone going to show that they exist?

1888

It is I. Heinrich Hertz. I have a way to test Maxwell's prediction.

I send electricity into the balls... to make them spark, of course.

Each time there is a big spark at the balls, the wire loop receives a wave and there is a little spark in the gap.

wire loop

Gosh! Energy is being transmitted across space.

the 1890s

I wonder if we could apply these Hertzian waves to carry messages? The length of the waves is so long they won't be reflected by trees or houses.

Je suis Eduard Branly

and I'm Oliver Lodge

You'll need a better receiver than that old wire loop – then if you change the pattern sent out you can see it at the receiver. A pattern of shorts and longs would let you signal in Morse code.

Ciao! I'm-a Guglielmo Marconi, and I'm gonna improve on Lodge's idea by making the generator better. I'll connect one side to earth and the other to a long wire. I'll call this an antenna.

Using more and more powerful generators, by 1901 Marconi was ready to send a message across the Atlantic.

Say, that's great! A message sent by radiation of waves. Let's call it 'radio' for short. Have a nice day.

Jolly good show. A message sent by telegraph without wires. Let's call it 'wireless' for short.

Cape Cod U.S.A.

Cornwall U.K.

1906

This stuff with spark gaps is old hat. Now if I could replace that with a system of high frequency alternating currents ... Much easier, and you could modulate the radio wave with a sound wave.

Reg Fessenden

You mean like this

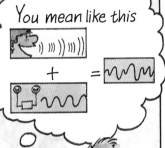

And so...

'Twas the night before Christmas...

Ah, yes! AM = Amplitude Modulation.

So now regular programmes could be broadcast, although improvements were still needed.

The year is 1921. The place is Pittsburgh, Pennsylvania. This is the World's first regular broadcast

Sounds awful! What they need is a woofer!

EXPLORE
- What was Maxwell's **prediction**?
- How did Hertz test this prediction?
- How was Hertz's discovery **applied**?
- How is Hertz's name used today in connection with radio? (Look up the frequency of some radio stations.)

TRAVELLING SOUND

Hearing things?

Have you ever noticed these things?

You see Concorde fly by before you hear it

You see lightning before you hear the thunder

Why do you think they happen? Here are some ideas.

> *Because your eyes are more sensitive than your ears.*

> *Light travels quicker than sound.*

> *It takes time for things to make a sound.*

> *Your brain notices pictures more quickly than sounds.*

EXPLORE

- Which ideas do you agree with? **Record** them and add some ideas of your own.

If you twang a ruler the air molecules move closer together or compress when the ruler moves forward ▼

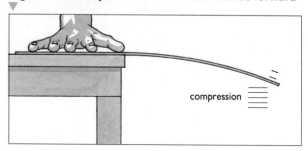

compression

The air molecules then move apart when the ruler moves back ▼

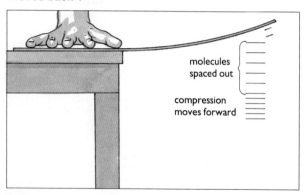

molecules spaced out

compression moves forward

Getting the vibes

You can hear sounds when **vibrations** reach your ears. ▼

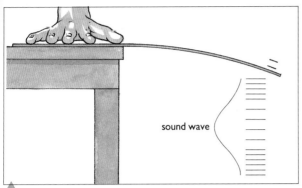

As the ruler moves back and forward more bits of air get compressed. This makes a sound wave

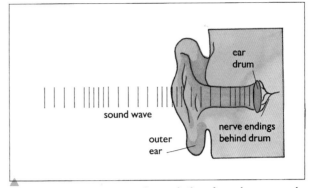

The sound wave moves through the air and may reach your ear

EXPLORE

- What do you think would happen if you used a thicker ruler?
- What would happen if you made the ruler shorter?
- What substance is the sound wave moving through?
- What energy changes are involved while sound gets from the ruler to your ear?

PRESENT

- Humming birds, bees and other insects make a buzzing sound with their wings. Collect pictures of animals that make sounds like this and make a poster showing how their wings buzz, and how we hear them. Include a diagram showing the energy changes that happen. You are **applying**.

Can you hear it?

EXPLORE

- What substance is the sound moving through in each diagram?
- What energy changes are involved in each situation?
- Why do you think you can't hear the bell ringing when all the air is taken out of the glass cylinder?
- Do you think you can hear things in outer space? Why?
- What substances does sound travel through easily?
- What things could you do to reduce the noise coming from the stereo? You are **applying**.

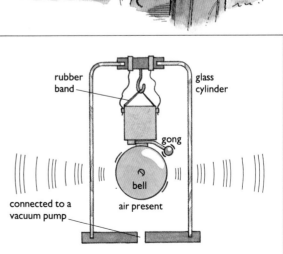

WAVES FROM THE SUN

What's in sunshine?

The Sun's rays are bright and hot. What makes them like that? Is there anything else in sunshine, that we can't see or feel?

Energy from the Sun comes in a variety of **waves** which are made by electrons vibrating. The waves all travel at the same speed, but the electrons vibrate at a higher **frequency** (more often) in some waves than others. For example, X-rays have a very high frequency, while radio waves have a low frequency. Waves with a high frequency have a short **wavelength** (distance from one wave to the next), while those with a low frequency have a long wavelength. Radio waves have a long wavelength.

All these waves make up a family called the **electromagnetic spectrum**.

EXPLORE

Look at the picture of the electromagnetic spectrum.
- Which waves have the longest wavelength?
- Which waves have the highest frequency?
- What is the wavelength of the waves we can see?

wavelength

**Wavelength is the distance from one wave to the next.
If you sat on a rock and counted the waves coming past ▲
you in a minute, you would know their frequency**

SUN'S WAVES COVER THE FULL SPECT

infrared waves

10^{-4}

10^{-5}

10^{-6}

ultraviolet waves

10^{-7}

10^{-8}

10^{-9}

visible light

electr

10^{-10}

gamma rays

10^{-11}

X-rays

10^{-12}

waves
with short
wavelengths

nuclear radiation

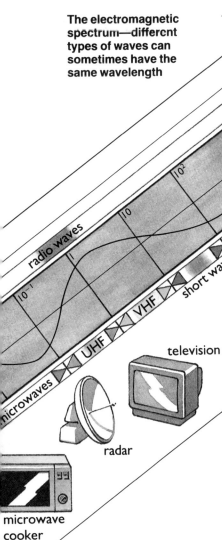

The electromagnetic spectrum—different types of waves can sometimes have the same wavelength

this scale shows wavelength (in metres)

10^4

waves with long wavelengths

10^3

10^2

10

long wave

medium wave

short wave

VHF

10^{-1}

UHF

radio waves

microwaves

radio

television

radar

microwave cooker

PRESENT

■ Make a collage of different types of electromagnetic waves. Cut Out LS10 will help. Include pictures from magazines showing how we use different waves.

Light you can see

You can only see a small part of the Sun's energy—we call this part **visible light**. If visible light goes through a glass prism, it is split up into different colours. This is because waves with short wavelengths are bent more by glass than waves with long wavelengths. Violet light has a shorter wavelength than red light.

This mnemonic will help you remember the colours in visible light: Richard Of York Gave Battle In Vain ▶

You see these colours in a rainbow—water in the air breaks up visible light into different wavelengths ▼

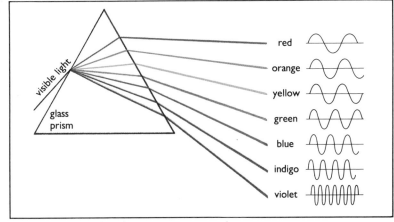

visible light

glass prism

red
orange
yellow
green
blue
indigo
violet

EXPLORE

■ A red jumper can't produce visible light, so how do you think it looks red? What do coloured objects do that makes them look the colour they do?

■ Black isn't in the spectrum of visible light—how do you think we see black?

INDEX

You'll notice that there are no page numbers in this book. The index refers to spread numbers.